Stalking the Spirit

Stalking the Spirit
In a Do-It-Yourself Church

MARJORY ZOET BANKSON

WIPF & STOCK · Eugene, Oregon

STALKING THE SPIRIT
In a Do-It-Yourself Church

Copyright © 2014 Marjory Zoet Bankson. All rights reserved. Except for brief quotations in critical publications or reviews, no part of this book may be reproduced in any manner without prior written permission from the publisher. Write: Permissions. Wipf and Stock Publishers, 199 W. 8th Ave., Suite 3, Eugene, OR 97401.

Wipf and Stock
An Imprint of Wipf and Stock Publishers
199 W. 8th Ave., Suite 3
Eugene, OR 97401

www.wipfandstock.com

ISBN 13: 978-1-62564-764-1

Manufactured in the U.S.A.   09/02/2014

With grateful thanks to all the Seekers, named and unnamed in this account, whose lives and stories have woven the fabric of our life together

Contents

Introduction | ix

1 **Family Heritage** | 1
  Roots in Church of the Saviour

2 **In the Beginning** | 14
  The Call of Seekers Church

3 **Shared Leadership** | 21
  Building a Loyal Core Group

4 **Spiritual Formation in Community** | 31
  Worship, Retreats, and Mission Groups

5 **Money as a Working Theology** | 43
  "Where Your Treasure Is . . ."

6 **Beliefs That Bind Us Together** | 51
  Reworking the Commitment Statement

7 **Open Pulpit** | 58
  The Spirit Speaks in Many Tongues

8 **Team Leadership** | 66
  Encouraging Commitment for All

9 **New Wineskins** | 78
  Reshaping Church of the Saviour

10 **Holding the Tension** | 89
  Letting the Creative Process Work

11 **New Leadership Emerges** | 102
  Transition to the Next Generation at Seekers

12 **Manna in the Desert** | 117
Disciplined by Waiting

13 **Home at Last!** | 125
Settling in at Carroll Street

14 **Practicing Ministry in Daily Life** | 135
Seekers Gathered and Sent

APPENDIX 1 *Membership Commitment of the Church of the Saviour* | 149

APPENDIX 2 *Call of Seekers Church (April 25, 1976)* | 151

APPENDIX 3 *Call of Seekers Church (September, 1976)* | 153

APPENDIX 4 *Seekers' Call (1989)* | 155

APPENDIX 5 *Stewards Commitment Statement* | 157

APPENDIX 6 *Disciplines of the Stewards* | 159

APPENDIX 7 *General Membership Statements* | 161

APPENDIX 8 *Books by Seekers* | 164

APPENDIX 9 *Questions for Emerging Churches* | 165

Bibliography | 171

Index | 173

Introduction

IN 1965 A FRIEND handed me an old copy of *Faith at Work* magazine, saying that we might find some good ideas for small groups in it. Instead, I found an article by Elizabeth O'Connor, "What We Need Is More Saints." It was my first introduction to Church of the Saviour, a small ecumenical church in Washington, DC. What caught my attention was her emphasis on the transformative possibilities of what she called "mission groups." In the article, Elizabeth wrote:

> We are seeking to bring people into the Christian community and not just to affect them individually, but to bring them into the Christian community which can mature them and bring them to the point of ministry. . . . We need to throw away the maps which we have used in the past, to know that we have capacities that we have not exercised. What happens to people under the stimulation of the Holy Spirit is that they discover that they have been living far beneath that of which they are capable.[1]

The notion that we have "capacities that we have not exercised," and that mission groups could combine spiritual growth with service, intrigued me. I longed for a place where commitment and social change danced together, but it would be several years before that was possible.

Our first taste of mission group life occurred in 1968, when my husband, Peter, and I moved to Hanover, New Hampshire. The local UCC church was sponsoring a coffeehouse patterned after The Potter's House, the first corporate mission of Church of the Saviour. Unlike many coffeehouses in the sixties, each night at The Potter's House was staffed by a committed team of people who shared an "inward journey" along with their service to others. Our local version in Hanover, The Ram's Horn, required that we sign a similar commitment to the inward/outward journey of mission group life when we joined the staff.

---

1. Faith at Work, October–November 1963, 37.

Introduction

The Ram's Horn staff was our first experience of intentional community with a common purpose, and we liked it a lot. Our work was to serve customers from the Dartmouth community with food and companionship during those turbulent years of student protest for civil rights and against the Vietnam War. Since we were there because of Peter's assignment to teach ROTC at Dartmouth, the coffeehouse felt like an island of sanity in a crazy and conflicted world.

At The Ram's Horn, our staff of six people met to share and pray for an hour before we opened the doors of the coffeehouse. Tempers often rose at the end of the evening when people wanted to get home, and the kitchen still needed to be mopped. Differences in personality, energy, and values created lots of tension, but our common commitment held us together. Our staff team studied Elizabeth O'Connor's books, *Call to Commitment* and *Journey Inward, Journey Outward*, hoping that she would guide us through some of our difficulties. To our disappointment, she didn't have many answers, except to focus on our sense of God's call, and to affirm each other's gifts.

Over time, we learned the rudiments of seeing gifts in each other, even as we struggled with keeping our disciplines of daily prayer, showing up on time, and staying until the work was finished. Some Dartmouth students wanted to join The Ram's Horn staff, but they often felt they couldn't commit to daily disciplines or regular service at the coffeehouse. Others objected to the word "Christian," in the commitment statement. While we were there, from 1968 to 1970, the manager was firm about the need for a full commitment. Later, the commitment statement was relaxed, staff reliability declined, and The Ram's Horn closed within a year. It was a lesson that we carried with us.

We moved to Washington, DC, in 1976, and by then we were ready to explore Church of the Saviour (C of S), no matter how far the commute would be. We found a house in Alexandria, Virginia, and moved in on Bicentennial Day, July 4, 1976. The following Sunday, we attended C of S for the first time. We were horrified to discover that the church was in the process of dividing into several smaller churches. How would we know which one to attend? Who was going to "get" Gordon Cosby, the founding pastor of Church of the Saviour? Or his gracious wife, Mary? Or the author we so admired, Elizabeth O'Connor?

In retrospect, God's timing could not have been better. What we initially saw as a chaotic breakup of C of S proved to be the creative swirl of

Introduction

new birth and new leadership for the second generation of churches that grew out of the original body.

Stalking the Spirit is the story of Seekers, one of the churches that emerged from the Church of the Saviour in 1976. As a do-it-yourself church, with no denominational affiliation, we have been free to develop structures to fit our sense of God's call as it has taken shape in the congregation over time.

There were three distinct periods. At first, we relied on the vision and leadership of our founding pastors, Fred Taylor and Sonya Dyer. They wrote the initial call of Seekers Church, and in the first decade focused on developing a loyal core group based on God's call to ministry in daily life. Their commitment to shared leadership made space for different calls and gifts to emerge within the church, as we moved from a singular focus on the ministry of Jesus, which characterized the parent church, to the more elusive guidance of the Holy Spirit.

The second phase of development was more organizational, and yet open to the Spirit as we sought to become a functioning body of Christ. When Fred resigned in 1988, the core members decided not to replace him on the staff team, but to open the pulpit to anyone who might feel called to "bring us the word" on Sunday. By then, a matrix of mission groups gave people a structure within Seekers for the inward/outward journey of service and belonging. The Celebration Circle mission group provided continuity in worship, with a seasoned liturgist to hold the space, so we could have a different person preaching each week. Another mission group sponsored our weeknight School of Christian Living, where people could sample the kind of commitment that mission groups provided. As the community grew to seventy adults and forty children, the core group also grew in numbers and shared leadership skills, although loving one another seemed harder as we struggled to find time for family, work, and mission group life too.

The third phase was marked by Sonya's departure and our move to a new location, on the northern edge of Washington, DC. When the nine C of S churches decided to sell the headquarters building, where we had worshipped since the beginning, Seekers had to find a new home. The challenge of staying together, finding a building that we could afford, raising money for the renovation, and settling in to a new neighborhood took a toll on our numbers, and toughened us up as well. In this more relational period, we had to trust individuals and smaller groupings with important

Introduction

decisions. We learned to trust the Spirit for timing on important decisions as well. The result today is a fairly resilient body of believers, growing diversity, and a generous heart.

As a lay-led body of Christ with no single pastor, our path of discovery might be helpful to other emerging congregations. Old patterns of being church seem to be cracking apart. There are no institutional guarantees of longevity. But if our experience can raise questions or widen the conversation among those who want to find meaning and ministry in the ordinary structures of our daily lives, I will have passed on the gift that Elizabeth O'Connor's article was to me.

Although I have lived through most of these events myself, I know my view is limited. I have had access to the complete minutes of monthly core group meetings, C of S records, liturgies and sermons dating back to 1976, journals and letters from Sonya Dyer and Muriel Lipp, and interviews with most of the early members. Sermons and other basic documents can be found on the website, www.seekerschurch.org. Knowing Seekers, I am sure there will be other interpretations that are equally valid. I can only say that I've done my best to tell the story with as much veracity as I can.

Marjory Zoet Bankson

1

Family Heritage
Roots in Church of the Saviour

ON SUNDAY, OCTOBER 5, 1946, Gordon and Mary Cosby met with seven others to begin Church of the Saviour as "a local expression of the universal church." A year later, that group made their first official commitment in response to what they felt to be God's call to become a deeply committed body of Christ together. Every year after that, a small but growing number of members would commit to those principles on the third Sunday of October, which became known as Recommitment Sunday.

Gordon's vision had been shaped by his experience as an army chaplain with the 101st Airborne Division in France during WWII. With so many facing imminent death, Gordon worked with volunteers at the squad level to help them minister to others. He wrote home to his wife, Mary, about his dream of building an ecumenical community of Christians who would truly love the world in all of its brokenness, as God did. Mary shared Gordon's vision, and together they became a complementary team as the church began to take shape after the war.

Gordon's preaching and teaching set the direction for everything at the church, and Mary's deep faith, sense of beauty, and gracious Southern hospitality welcomed all who came. Together, they nurtured a community based on God's call and their commitment to it. Administrative support for Gordon's visionary leadership came in 1948, when the small group of church members purchased an old rooming house at 1707 19th Street NW. As Gordon often said, "We bought Bill Branner along with the church building." Bill moved across the street from the new church, married

Sunshine Ferguson, and became Gordon's partner in ministry as the financial manager. For the next fifty years, Bill Branner provided counsel to the many different missions that grew out of Church of the Saviour, so they could organize and incorporate as separate non-profit organizations.

Church of the Saviour (C of S) put down deeper roots in the city when a substantial brownstone at 2025 Massachusetts Avenue NW was purchased in 1950 for $60,000—a sizable debt for just 19 members with an average per capita income of $200/month. To lighten the interior, members painted the walnut paneling apple green, and Mary Cosby's mother added a mural in the front office and on the dining room wall to cover the wall cracks. Fondly known as "2025," the brownstone served as the worship center. Money for maintenance of 2025 was always a low priority, and it stayed that way as missions began to emerge for healing the city of racism and poverty.

As the culture of America became increasingly noisy with the spread of television in the early fifties, Church of the Saviour called people to silence and contemplation in the tradition of Quakers and some Roman Catholic orders. The plain, unadorned chapel at 2025 was meant to focus attention on God. Emphasis on silent retreat grew from Gordon's firm conviction that ministry flows from a wellspring of "divine oneness," best experienced in communal silence. That became known as "the journey inward."

Dreams for a retreat center took shape in 1952, when three young women from the church began scouting for a place of respite and renewal in the country. They found a 170-acre farm near Gaithersburg, Maryland, which was for sale. The Easter offering brought a down payment of $9,000 for what became known as the Dayspring Farm. Plans were drawn for a lodge to host day-long silent retreats, which was built with dedicated but largely unskilled labor by the church members. Muriel Lipp, who became one of the founding members of Seekers Church, remembers going to Dayspring every weekend with her young family to clear stones and picnic together with other members of C of S in those early days.

PREPARING ALL MEMBERS FOR MINISTRY

Gordon was strongly influenced by Dietrich Bonhoeffer's writings, and every person who came into membership at C of S spent time with Bonhoeffer's book *Life Together*. In it, Bonhoeffer warned against human efforts at community because the way would be blocked by our ego needs. Only Christ, he wrote, could release us from "the wishful notion of religious fellowship" and open us to genuine relationship through acknowledgment that we are all sinners. Beyond listening deeply and hearing one another's confession, Bonhoeffer described the ministry of bearing one another's burdens as the primary call to love the world toward wholeness. His focus was on shaping disciples through confession, care, accountability, and service. That became the central purpose of each mission group.

In addition to Saturday work parties at Dayspring and Sunday worship at 2025, many prospective members attended the weeknight School of Christian Living. Mary and Gordon, along with Mary's sister, Elizabeth Anne Campagna, taught regularly at the school. Elizabeth O'Connor arrived at Church of the Saviour in 1952 and quickly became involved at the school, teaching classes and guiding groups. She soon joined Gordon and Bill as the only paid staff members of the church. Later, her books became the way that people beyond Washington, DC, learned about this unique body of Christ. Over time, Elizabeth became the primary interpreter of Gordon's prophetic ministry through her books.

Challenging preparation for membership was meant to equip everyone for local ordination and service in the world. Every prospective member was expected to complete five classes in the School, give proportionately of one's income, join a mission group, work with a confirmed member as a sponsor, and finally, write a spiritual autobiography which would be shared upon coming into full membership. It also made yearly recommitment a soul-searching exercise.

Speaking at a meeting of the World Council of Churches in 1958, Gordon pursued the theme of ministry for all persons. "The distinction between laity and clergy," he said, "tends to perpetuate the feeling of a second-class order in the church."[1] He described the Church of the Saviour practice of ordaining each member for ministry as recognition that he or she had been "grasped by God" for a task that "the church must have done." That work was to address the pockets of pain and injustice as Jesus might have, with love and healing.

FIRST MISSION

Although every member of Church of the Saviour was committed to personal disciplines and some form of collective outreach, it was hard for covenant groups to decide what their shared mission would be. As Elizabeth

---

1. Cosby, *By Grace Transformed*, 37.

O'Connor described in her book *Servant Leaders, Servant Structures*, the first corporate call came through a chance encounter that Gordon and Mary had while on a church visit in 1959. They found their host church cold and stiff, but at a country inn where they stayed, the tavern below their room seemed warm and friendly. When they returned to Washington, Gordon and Mary were ready to "sound a call" for their first corporate mission through a coffee house in the inner city.

When The Potter's House, a coffeehouse and bookstore on Columbia Road, finally opened in 1960, it was staffed each night by a different mission group. Each group was led by a moderator, who would serve as a *pastor/prophet*, and a *spiritual director*, who received a weekly written report from members of the group. In practice, the moderator usually kept an eye on the outward mission or task of the group, while the spiritual director gave pastoral attention to the group members. With that in place, mission groups became the primary place of accountability and relationship for church members, while Gordon's preaching provided challenge and direction for the whole community.

Rather than functioning with a committee structure, Church of the Saviour grew organically as new mission groups formed around a written call that was shared by at least two core members. By 1961 there were seventy committed members, and roughly three times that number attending the two Sunday services at the brownstone or the lay-led service at The Potter's House. The coffeehouse ministry was a year old, and the mission groups keeping it open five nights a week were both exuberant and exhausted. Elizabeth O'Connor sounded a note of concern about the proliferation of mission groups with a small pamphlet titled "A Precarious Hour." In it, she questioned whether all the mission groups could really do the challenging inner work of healing and spiritual formation.

At that time, Elizabeth was working in the office of the church, and trying to write her first book, *Call to Commitment*. Attracted to the depth psychology of Carl Jung, Elizabeth offered classes in the school that would pass for group therapy in many other places. Elizabeth's second book, *Journey Inward, Journey Outward* (1968), detailed the necessity for regular self-examination and prayer to sustain outward mission. Those published books gave her a voice of authority within the C of S community and beyond. Through them, O'Connor reached a wide audience and established her place as the official interpreter of what was happening at Church of the Saviour.

SEEDBED FOR SEEKERS

During the sixties, Washington, DC, seethed with the tumult of civil rights and anti-war activism. With a black majority population, the District government struggled for federal money and home rule against a range of entrenched white power structures. Racism ruled without much question. After school integration was mandated by *Brown vs. Board of Education*, activists in the District pressed for school integration, and white flight to the suburbs undercut efforts to do it without violence.

In March of 1965, Gordon traveled to Selma, Alabama, to march with Dr. Martin Luther King Jr. and other leaders from the Southern Christian Leadership Conference. More than forty ministers from the Washington area chartered a flight, and joined hundreds of others from around the country in the growing civil rights movement. On that trip, Gordon agreed with five other local ministers that they needed to do something right there in Washington, DC. One logical target was Junior Village, a residential facility that housed unwanted or neglected children in deplorably crowded conditions. On the Sunday following his return, Gordon issued a challenge to the congregation:

> Junior Village should be eliminated! There are almost 1,000 children there, being denied that which a child must have and we sit around and watch. . . . I would like to challenge you to so live with God until you find that some segment of the city is laid on your heart and you'll not rest until you help make it whole.[2]

Those who responded to Gordon's call formed a new mission group, For Love of Children (FLOC), whose purpose was to attack the problem of neglected children in the nation's capital. Gordon imagined small, dedicated groups of five or ten people in Catholic, Protestant, and Jewish congregations, each supporting about five children from Junior Village. Through the summer of 1965, Sunday afternoon meetings were held at 2025 to inform and encourage an effort to contact nearly 1,300 congregations in the city, and to find prospective homes for the children in Junior Village.

Fred Taylor, who later became one of the cofounders of Seekers, was a Baptist minister with Southern roots who came to one of those early meetings. Even though he had a young family in the suburbs, he resigned from his church in northern Virginia and was eager to get involved. Within the year, Fred was hired to be FLOC's first director. His office was at the

---

2. Cosby, *By Grace Transformed*, 182.

headquarters building for Church of the Saviour, so he had daily interactions with Gordon and Elizabeth O'Connor as FLOC began to develop as the first separately incorporated mission out of C of S.

FLOC volunteers from different churches literally went from door to door in the District, asking for homes in which to place children from Junior Village. Although results were slow, FLOC discovered a few families who wanted to retrieve their own children from Junior Village, and began to work with them.

Hope and a Home began as a FLOC mission group, to work with eight specific families, including some fifty children, twenty of whom had been at Junior Village. Sonya Dyer, a neighborhood activist from northern Virginia, joined the Hope and a Home mission group soon after it formed. She persuaded her friend, Emily Benson, to get involved too. Although Sonya and Emily lived in the predominantly white suburbs, their experiences in the city would be formative for Seekers.

Following Martin Luther King Jr.'s assassination in 1968, riots catalyzed a new sense of mission for those at Church of the Saviour. Although the headquarters building, on Massachusetts Avenue, was not in the riot corridor, the Adams Morgan neighborhood around The Potter's House was heavily damaged. When the C of S mission groups decided to keep The Potter's House open through that time, they put down firmer roots in the city. FLOC, and the Hope and a Home mission group, was another expression of that commitment.

By 1969 there were approximately one hundred people involved in different FLOC groups. Many were unfamiliar with the emphasis on an "inward journey" that was common at Church of the Saviour, but they were eager to help with the FLOC programs. As the Executive Director of FLOC, Fred was charged with receiving spiritual reports from those C of S members who were involved in FLOC, so, in practice, he became their spiritual director. Fred recognized that FLOC's rapid expansion was creating real conflict with the disciplined spiritual life that C of S wanted in its mission groups, but his call to FLOC remained expansive and inclusive of people from other congregations. During that tumultuous period, Sonya began to function as a bridge builder between the C of S members of FLOC and the congregation at 2025. Because both Sonya and Fred had teenagers at home, balancing home and family with the challenges of inner-city ministry became a focus for both of them.

MISSION GROUP ORTHODOXY

Gordon's preaching, Mary's teaching, and Elizabeth's books continued to draw newcomers to Church of the Saviour. Although mission groups at Potter's House served to deepen the inward/outward journey of their members, a number of other counseling and "inventory" groups had also formed without a disciplined inner life or a commitment to serving "the poor."

In 1969, Elizabeth O'Connor noted the unsettling news that 25 percent of the approximately seventy-five C of S committed members were in no group at all. In response, Gordon risked a mass exodus from membership by suspending the annual recommitment service until the requirements for membership could be clarified. Shortly after that, O'Connor outlined these requirements and announced formation of a more formal council that would be made up of representatives *only from groups with a corporate or shared mission*, starting with those named below:

Each member of C of S would practice these inner disciplines:

- Meet God daily in a set time of prayer.
- Let God confront us daily through the Scripture.
- Worship weekly—normally with our Church.
- Give proportionately, beginning at a tithe of our income.

Only confirmed mission groups would have a representative on the Council, which would be the governing board of the Church:

- Dag Hammarskjold College
- Children's Education
- Kittamaqundi (Columbia, MD)
- Retreat (Dayspring)
- Vineyard Workers
- Shepherds (School of Christian Living)
- FLOC: Hope and a Home
- Potter's House Tuesday Group
- Potter's House Wednesday Group
- Potter's House Thursday Group
- Potter's House Friday Group
- Potter's House Saturday Group
- CoffeeHouse Church

> The School of Christian Living would provide orientation to the whole concept of Christian life and mission and it would strengthen mission groups. The Council could designate one or more courses to be required prior to joining a mission group.

Listing the "confirmed mission groups" documented the importance of Potter's House, with six representatives. FLOC had only one. The council would meet every other month with the C of S staff, rotating representatives from those mission groups so that every member would sit on the council at some point. Although the process was designed to share the council experience, it also meant that nobody developed enough expertise to discuss policy or provide functional oversight for the staff. In this configuration, the council could not be a governing board. Instead, it became a distribution center for staff initiatives.

GROWTH PRECIPITATES CHANGE

Elizabeth O'Connor's books continued to support and guide mission group life toward ongoing spiritual formation for all members. In 1971, *Our Many Selves* described how awareness of wounds and blockages keep us from receiving the love of God. A second book, *Eighth Day of Creation: Gifts and Creativity*, contained a series of meditations for discovering gifts for ministry along with a powerful section on how we bury our gifts for fear of having to take responsibility for them. In 1972, the third book of this trilogy came out as *Search for Silence*, in which she outlined how meditation and contemplation rooted in Scripture could open one to God's guidance and direction. These three books became the standard curriculum for teaching spiritual growth at the School of Christian Living.

As new mission groups formed, the C of S Council kept expanding. FLOC added mission groups for a Wilderness School and a Learning Center. Those interested in housing purchased two dilapidated buildings near The Potter's House, the Ritz and the Mozart, and soon Jubilee Housing spawned Jubilee Neighbors and Literacy Action. Potter's House added the Polycultural Institute and a mission group for Senior Communities. At Dayspring Farm, the Wellspring mission group formed to expose visitors to the inward and outward dimensions of call at Church of the Saviour. Mission groups tried to operate by consensus, but the council, made up of mission group representatives, had neither the time nor the inner connection to do that, so it became something of a rubber stamp for whatever the C of S staff proposed.

In July of 1974 Gordon shocked the entire community when he shared with the council his own changing sense of call. He cited the rapid growth in numbers and proliferation of ministries as the cause for his proposal—to divide into three smaller worshiping centers. True to his vision that churches must form around God's call to be a living body of Christ, Gordon suggested mission clusters around the three existing worshipping communities: at 2025 Massachusetts Avenue, at The Potter's House, and at Dayspring.

In response to Gordon's challenge, the council decided to select nine people from the four different major mission groupings—The Potter's House, FLOC, Jubilee Housing, and Dayspring—for what they called the New Lands Servant Group. Sonya and Fred were selected to represent FLOC. The New Lands Group was to meet regularly until they could come back to the council with a proposal. In those meetings, Sonya spoke out about the hierarchy of mission groups represented on the council, with some getting much more staff attention than others. In her journal, Sonya wrote that "work and celebration had become unbalanced" and, "given the complexity of our private lives, there was little recognition for the demands of raising a family as mission." She thought the real issues were "family vs. mission, leadership style, and financial stewardship." Later, those issues would later become central in forming Seekers.

Muriel Lipp, who had been sponsored into C of S membership by Elizabeth O'Connor, submitted a paper to the New Lands Group urging a new definition of mission that would include one's job:

> My feeling about our mission structure is that it is much too narrow to allow full expression of the great diversity of gifts in our congregation. I cannot imagine that the score of missions expresses mission for all of our people. Or are people squeezing themselves into structures because that is the only way to belong? How does a doctor view mission? Isn't his profession his mission? Shouldn't we have a group for the expression of individual mission? I can't really believe that the mission meeting they attend once a week, whether Potter's House or whatever, is their expression of mission? Isn't a person's job also a call? We have many people in our church who have taken jobs within our church structure in order to express call, but those of us in secular structures feel this need too.

Muriel's letter touched a sore spot in the body of Church of the Saviour. Some members did indeed have paying jobs within the church structure. Muriel's job, teaching learning-disabled children in a public school, felt like call to her, but she was expected to join a mission group with another mission in order to qualify for membership.

Muriel suggested a more diffused style of collective leadership using "elders," joy and celebration with whole families, more intimacy through shared stories, and reinforcement for a simple lifestyle. She also imagined a fellowship of members that would meet regularly to share leadership of a new community. That would become the model adopted by Seekers.

SOURCE OF THE NAME

In the middle of this creative chaos, Robert Greenleaf's essay, "Being a Seeker in the Late 20th Century," was published in *Friends Journal*, a monthly magazine of Quaker life and thought. As a lifelong Quaker and retired AT&T executive, Greenleaf had a lot of credibility when he began to write about servant leadership, and his work was highly regarded at Church of the Saviour. This particular article touched Fred Taylor and Sonya Dyer at a crucial time. In it, Greenleaf wrote:

> The variable that marks some periods as barren and some as rich in prophetic vision is in the interest, the level of seeking, the responsiveness of the hearers. . . . It is SEEKERS, then, who make the prophet; and the initiative of any one of us in searching for and responding to the voice of the contemporary prophet may mark the turning point in his or her growth and service.

Greenleaf pointed to the integrity of Alcoholics Anonymous with its network of mutual support through deep listening. He suggested an organization of servant leaders to be called Seekers Anonymous, and he concluded his article with these stirring words: "By their intense and sustained listening they will make the new prophet who will help them find that wholeness that is only achieved by serving."

In response to this article, Fred insisted that Robert Greenleaf be invited to meet with the New Lands Group. When he came, Greenleaf commented that their language and logic were "inadequate for the task" before them. He questioned their bias toward smallness, and observed a lack of trust within the group. He challenged them to address the difference between centralized leadership (C of S staff) and a more democratic style of leadership in the mission groups. Greenleaf also noted that the council, made up of changing representatives from the mission groups, had no common life together, and he cautioned that council members were essentially competing for the resources of C of S staff time and attention.

By Christmas of 1975, the New Lands Group had two options on the table. One, articulated by Elizabeth O'Connor, proposed that the church exist in diaspora—that all properties of Church of the Saviour be sold and the staff dispensed with, except for those needed to organize a yearly gathering of small, disciplined mission groups. The other scenario, articulated by Wes Granberg-Michaelson, the secretary for the New Lands Group and later the General Secretary for the Reformed Church of America, was to form three congregations around existing worship centers: Jubilee, which would be the congregation at 2025; Potter's House, to be located at the coffeehouse, and Lifespring, which would include the Wellspring mission group, the silent retreat group at Dayspring Farm, and FLOC. Although the FLOC office was still located at the C of S headquarters building, and would logically have become part of the Jubilee congregation, FLOC was included in Lifespring because of its focus on outdoor education for inner-city youth.

On January 18, 1976, the New Lands Group reported to the council that they had reached consensus on a description of what would constitute a C of S community, and they did not try to determine how the members would congregate:

> Our Call must be our starting point. That call is to build a community centered in resolute faithfulness to Jesus Christ. It is to be His body, molded by His spirit. That call encompasses the marks which our community has discovered to be true and essential to its identity as God's people.
>
> Each community's call would have four thrusts:
> - to be Christ's church throughout the world—we are part of the ecumenical church, and want to give ourselves to it;
> - to the poor and oppressed—we believe that Christ calls us as His disciples to give ourselves to the oppressed of the world, especially those in our own city;
> - to the stranger in our midst—we are called to bring Christ's love to all those whose lives intersect with ours at any point; and

- to the building of our common life—all else must flow from our call to be God's people, celebrating our oneness with Him and nurturing ourselves as Christ's body.

The marks of each community would be:

- a corporate commitment to spiritual disciplines;
- mission groups would be the primary crucible for spiritual formation;
- for sacrificial outpouring together in mission to the brokenness of the world.

The New Lands Report was adopted at a rare congregational meeting of all C of S members, and the stage was set for the formation of new churches around the guidelines set forth above.

Very quickly, new churches then began to coalesce as people stepped forward to offer leadership. Mary Hitchcock shared her interest in pastoring at Potter's House. Dayspring printed its first newsletter as a sign that it had begun to see itself as a separate church, and Fred Taylor approached Sonya Dyer about calling a church from their experience at FLOC.

At that time, Fred and Sonya were both participating in the early service at 2025, although their children had outgrown the Sunday school there. They thought other families with children might be drawn to their vision for a separate church at 2025, so they did not pursue the suggestion that they join with others at the Dayspring property, which was a forty-five-minute drive from 2025. They chose Seekers as the name because they hoped to call forth new prophets by creating an environment for deep listening, as Greenleaf had suggested in his article, "Becoming a Seeker in the Late 20th Century."

Looking back on thirty years of being a single body as Church of the Saviour, the outlines of faithfulness to Gordon and Mary's original vision are clear. Gordon's preaching had inspired a culture of radical commitment, expressed through mission groups, each with a specific outward focus for healing the city. Mary's teaching at the School of Christian Living about God's call, and her generous embrace of everyone, brought a gracious sense of community and purpose at 2025. Elizabeth O'Connor's writing publicized C of S to a whole generation of lay and clergy leaders throughout the country, and her books became the staple of classes at the school, which had successfully introduced a generation of members to ongoing biblical study and spiritual disciplines. Silent retreats were firmly established at

Family Heritage

Dayspring, to ground the "outward journey" in a life of prayer and oneness with God. How that would be transmitted by the churches that were emerging from the parent body remained to be seen.

2

In the Beginning
The Call of Seekers Church

IN CONTRAST TO THE singular leadership of Gordon Cosby, the mission group pattern of shared leadership informed Fred Taylor and Sonya Dyer when they began working on their vision for a second-generation church within the Church of the Saviour (C of S) tradition. As the founding pastors, they wrote the original call for Seekers Church, and then circulated it among the members of C of S to see who might respond.

Their understanding of call had both individual and collective dimensions. In the biblical tradition, Sonya and Fred understood God's call as an invitation to each individual for some specific purpose. They were, themselves, responding to such a call. The radical vision that had drawn people to Church of the Saviour in earlier years was also based on Paul's writing in the New Testament about becoming a body of Christ together. At C of S, each mission group formed around the call and commitment of at least two core members, who would hold the inward and outward dimensions of their work together, while all members developed deeper connections as a body.

Although Church of the Saviour always emphasized call over credentials, Fred brought considerable credibility to his position at Seekers. A graduate of Vanderbilt and Yale Divinity School, Fred was ordained as a Southern Baptist minister and had served a local Baptist church. By 1976, he had also spent a decade as the director of FLOC, leading the fight to close Junior Village. Because the FLOC office was in the C of S headquarters building at 2025 Mass. Ave., Fred had a good working relationship with Gordon. Fred's wife, Anne, was the part-time business manager at The Potter's House at that time, and their four children had been shaped by C of

S too. At forty-four, Fred was ready to share his passion for social change, and he was eager for a place to preach regularly in addition to his full-time work at FLOC.

Sonya was a college graduate with no formal theological education. She came to C of S from a traditional Presbyterian church in Arlington, Virginia, ready for a partnership of equals. Already a strong feminist, she had been active in neighborhood Catholic-Protestant dialogues following Vatican II, and she was interested in the liturgical reforms that were bringing lay people into greater visibility everywhere. Sonya's husband, Manning, was a local businessman and member of a Potter's House mission group. At forty-seven, with their three children launched, Sonya wrote in her journal:

> I feel that I bring gifts of pastoring, of being able to listen.... I see myself as an energizer and evoker more than a visionary, as a clarifier and partner more than an independent prophet and dreamer. ... I am also energized toward an increased understanding and appreciation of Eucharist.

OUTLINE OF SEEKERS' CALL

From the outset, Fred and Sonya agreed that God's call for Seekers could be expressed at home or at work as well as through the traditional C of S mission groups. Through their involvement with FLOC, both Fred and Sonya had a passion for children and youth in the nation's capital, as well as the children in their own families. Both were facing years of college expense for their own children, and they were keenly aware of other young parents, drawn by the vision of Church of the Saviour, who saw their daily work as call and vocation, but they dismissed the idea that FLOC would be their corporate mission because they felt that a single mission was "too small for any church."

Together, Fred and Sonya hammered out a basic vision for their new community. They began with the inward journey, expressed as the necessity for daily practice of individual disciplines. The middle section put emphasis on community life, on participatory worship, and on financial responsibility as a spiritual matter. By adopting the traditional concept of tithing 10 percent of one's income, Fred and Sonya continued the C of S expectation of sacrificial giving by all committed members, but they also made room for review and adjustment based on changing circumstances. Sonya said later that *flexibility* and *intentionality* were their financial guidelines. The final section described outward mission quite differently from the C of S orthodoxy of a single corporate mission to serve the poor. Instead, they claimed "ministry in daily life."

Fred and Sonya were ready to share their call at the C of S council meeting in April 1976. They suggested that "the seekers community" might be a servant community to other Washington churches, just as Wellspring would be a servant community to churches outside of Washington. The call broadened the C of S definition of mission to include work, family, and citizenship. It emphasized worship more than mission, shared leadership rather than one's individual call, and it clearly stated a feminist critique of dehumanizing social structures:

> The seekers community would see itself called into God's liberation vision for the world by honestly facing and being involved at those *tension points* which our pluralistic world creates. An example of this would be the demand of blacks, the poor and women, for justice and partnership in a heretofore affluent, white, male-dominated society . . . systems which dehumanize children. Other examples of tension points are *differing life styles*, marriage and family life.[1]

In the parent church, justice and reconciliation were much more focused on racial issues than on sexual orientation, but for Seekers, feminist concerns about the role of women in society broadened into a specific welcome for those who had been marginalized by society because of their sexual orientation. Muriel Lipp clarified the term "*differing life styles*" as Seekers' welcome for gay and lesbian members. By then, both she and the Dyers were aware that they had lesbian relatives, and Fred agreed that sexual discrimination was one of society's "dehumanizing structures." Mary Clare Powell, who became one of the founding members of Seekers, was also living openly with a female partner.

EMERGING CHURCHES

Instead of the three groupings suggested by the New Lands Report, there were actually five other communities besides Seekers beginning to emerge among the C of S members: Dayspring, at the C of S retreat farm; Dunamis

---

1. Appendix 2.

In the Beginning

Vocations, for discerning call in the workplace; Eighth Day, for a polycultural experience; Jubilee, with its focus on inner-city housing; and The Potter's House, already a coffeehouse on Columbia Road.

No vote was taken by the C of S council on the Seekers call at the April meeting because of questions that the council had about their lack of a single mission, so Fred and Sonya continued to rework the language of Seekers' call and gathered support among C of S members who were attending worship at one of the two services at 2025.

As community calls were confirmed by the council, there were several orphan mission groups that did not identify with one of the emerging churches. Muriel Lipp, whose letter is quoted above, belonged to Literacy Action, one of those orphan groups. The challenge for Muriel was that Church of the Saviour expected her to be in a mission group on top of a job that she saw as mission. By June, Muriel was ready to become a founding member of Seekers, where her job and her writing would be valued as part of God's call and her commitment to it.

SEEKERS' FOCUS

When the council met again in May, the minutes record a request from Seekers to take over the early service on Sunday mornings at 2025. As moderator of the council, Gordon expressed his approval of Seekers' request, and the council gave its blessing for the first Seekers service at 2025 on June 13. Prior to that first worship service, this description of Seekers was sent to prospective members:

> Seekers Mission: to be church
> - to live as a witnessing community to the good news of Christ.
> - to bring our whole selves (family, job, gifts, relationships, mission calls)
> - to include children with emphasis on their participation in all aspects
>
> Acting out our mission:
> 1. Covenant for individual and corporate scripture study, prayer, accountability (both time and financial) and annual recommitment;
> 2. Spending time in silence to discern the Spirit's direction;

Stalking the Spirit

3. Shared leadership in all aspects of church life;
4. Commit to openness and sharing of feelings, positive and negative, to bring our whole selves to church;
5. Equipping and supporting one another in the basic structures in which we live out our lives;
6. Specifically involve ourselves in mission centered around the tension points of our world;
7. Reflecting periodically on where we are, how we have arrived there and where we choose to move.

The phrase "acting out our mission" was designed to allay fears that Seekers would simply gather for worship and not continue C of S emphasis on inner growth and outward service. Claiming "shared leadership in all aspects of church life" was a radically different pattern from Gordon's dominant leadership in the parent church, but there was nothing in this letter about accountability through mission groups—because there were no mission groups in Seekers at that time.

FIRST BUDGET

Although not yet an approved church, C of S members who were attracted to Seekers met to create a separate budget for Seekers. In the parent church, the budget was simply presented to the council by the C of S staff. In Seekers, it would be developed together by the committed members. Prospectively, fifteen to twenty core members would join Seekers, so the group planned a budget based on their anticipated tithes. They knew other people would contribute, but core members could count on the tradition of sacrificial giving, so they made a wild guess that Seekers could plan for a total budget of $25,000.

The first budget at Seekers was divided into three categories: space, inreach, and outreach. They decided to allocate 20 percent for space (as a gift to C of S in lieu of rent). The more important issue was whether to pay Sonya and Fred, and if so, how much. Members finally decided to pay Fred 20 percent of his FLOC salary in return for one day per week of his time. Sonya would be paid an equal amount for whatever time she put in. It was a clear statement of support for their male/female, lay/clergy partnership, even though it was also apparent that Sonya would be spending more time on Seekers than Fred, who still had a full-time job as the director of

FLOC. Stipends for Fred and Sonya were designated as "inreach," equal to 40 percent of the budget. Balancing inreach and outreach became known as "the 50-50 rule," and it has remained a guideline for outreach giving by Seekers since then.

WOULD SEEKERS QUALIFY?

When the C of S council met in September of 1976 to consider the call of Seekers again, Fred and Sonya reassured the council that while Seekers had no single corporate mission to the oppressed, it would uphold the shared commitment to an inward and outward journey by all members. After much discussion over Seekers' lack of a single, defining corporate mission, the council decided to trust the leadership and commitment of Fred and Sonya because of FLOC and their participation in the New Lands Group.

The call of Seekers had been softened considerably from the strongly worded attack on the "white male system" that Fred and Sonya had originally drafted. Instead, there was a single sentence: *"The seekers community sees itself called into Christ's ministry of deliverance from bondage to freedom in every personal and corporate expression."*[2]

OFFICIAL LAUNCH

Yearly recommitment, on the third Sunday of October, marked the official launch of six new second-generation C of S churches in 1976. A total of seventy-seven members joined the sister communities: Dayspring (11), Dunamis Vocations (4), Eighth Day (18), Jubilee (17), Potter's House (8), and Seekers (19). Dayspring met for worship in the farmhouse at Dayspring Farm. Dunamis and Seekers worshiped at 2025 Mass. Ave. Eighth Day, Jubilee, and Potter's House met on different nights at The Potter's House, and many of those people also attended the ecumenical service at 2025 on Sunday mornings, where Gordon continued to preach. In addition, thirty-one members renewed their membership in C of S through unaffiliated mission groups. Everyone used the original C of S commitment statement, and the orphan groups were expected to affiliate with one of the new churches within the next year. Most did, although both Wellspring and Gateway remained as independent C of S mission groups until Gordon retired.

2. Appendix 3.

For Seekers, the call to ministry in daily life made it unique among the sister churches. The others claimed a single defining mission, but Fred and Sonya drew inspiration from their experience at FLOC and recognized that family, work, and citizenship might also be a call for some. All of the core members at Seekers had been through the preparation for membership required by Church of the Saviour, and understood themselves to be ordained for ministry. Each core member was in a mission group located somewhere within Church of the Saviour or FLOC, so building their identity as Seekers would be part of the effort to establish Seekers as a separate church. As pastoral partners, building a loyal core group would be the focus for Fred and Sonya as the new church formed.

3

Shared Leadership
Building a Loyal Core Group

Recalling the critique by Robert Greenleaf during the New Lands process, Sonya and Fred wanted Seekers to create structures that would be adequate to the task of supporting ministry in daily life. Both valued worship as an experience of the "church gathered," because members were so scattered during the week. Both recognized their need to develop a core group of those who would understand themselves as members of Seekers rather than Church of the Saviour. Being part-time also made it essential for Fred and Sonya to engage the core members in sharing leadership within the community. That began to happen as new mission groups formed within Seekers.

STALKING THE SPIRIT

Altering the worship space at the C of S headquarters building (2025) was the first sign that Seekers wanted to embrace a theology of Pentecost, of gifts poured out on many. At the early service, different people worked with Sonya to create symbols of the liturgical season for the altar, and to make bulletins that symbolized a community in dialogue with Spirit. They also moved the chairs into semi-circular rows for the early service and back again into straight rows for the second service, where Gordon would be preaching. These intentional changes felt purposeful and a bit subversive, marking Seekers as a separate body, intent on claiming new gifts for worship and service in a more inclusive way.

Each week, Fred and Sonya held the worship space together, as a sign that the Spirit was working in the space between them—that neither one embodied a single authority figure, as Jesus had. Out of his Southern Baptist background, Fred understood preaching as the highlight of the service, and he worked hard to make his sermons a call to liberation for everyone. Sonya's interest in liturgy as a formation process was expressed by her presence as the liturgist, rather than dividing the preaching with Fred as she might have. Sonya wrote her pastoral prayers with attention to current events in the city and in the world, and she held extended silent spaces in which prayers might be spoken from the congregation. Together, they held worship as a crucible for the Spirit to move in and through the gathered body.

Sonya was also outspoken in her refusal to limit the notion of shared leadership to co-pastoring with Fred. She invited intentional partnership in leading different activities, like writing the liturgy or developing ideas for including children. She asked interested people to choose music, develop special liturgies, and make bulletin covers for each liturgical season. She held a strong vision for sharing leadership as a way to let the Spirit call forth new gifts within the community, and without Sonya's commitment to involving others, it would not have happened.

Like Gordon, Fred was used to leading worship himself, so it was a big step for him to share the pulpit space with Sonya as he did. When we first came to Seekers in 1976, I wept as I saw them standing at the Communion table, blessing the elements together and then sharing them around the standing circle of worshipers. My tears told me how hungry I was to see the whole image of God, male and female, represented at the altar. By then I was thirty-seven years old and had lived in eight states and two foreign countries, but I had never seen a woman presiding at Communion!

METAPHORS FOR SEEKERS

Finding an image for Seekers began with designing a letterhead. Even though the address on the stationery was the same as Church of the Saviour, the letterhead said "The Seekers: A Church of the Saviour Faith Community." There was some discussion of putting several boats on the letterhead to indicate that Seekers was on a spiritual journey, rather than being a people who "had arrived," but in the end, the letterhead was left clean of symbols. The image of Seekers as a flotilla of separate little boats was also suggested on a bulletin cover drawn by another founding member, Harriette Mohr. She named the uncomfortable truth that "some have not made a firm commitment," and expressed that on the back of a bulletin cover for all to see. Whereas Elizabeth O'Connor had been the primary interpreter of Church of the Saviour, shared leadership at Seekers meant that there were many people describing the emerging metaphors for Seekers as people on a journey of discovery.

Another image for Seekers emerged from a ritual for receiving new members. When Carol Fitch, from the Wellspring mission group, was ready to join Seekers, Emily Benson designed a simple ritual involving Swedish ivy, rooted from a plant grown by another founding member. The pot had been used before, the soil came from a compost pile mixed with Ash Wednesday ashes, and the plant symbolized our willingness to be planted in space and time. It would need pruning and repotting in the future. It was also a visible statement of our theology, as a living, growing organism. As a professional potter, I was soon asked to make a special "membership pot." In keeping with the themes we had been hearing, I made it with a cut design of waves and circles. Since then, the soil has been depleted and replaced, the plant has sometimes died in the hands of a non-gardener, and still the cuttings thrive in many homes as a living symbol of Seekers as a community of endings and new beginnings.

At the same time, I also made a Communion set for Seekers that picked up the theme of water and waves on the bread plates and offering bowl, along with more than a hundred small individual cups, each one different. In my journal, I wrote about the symbolism this way: "These cups are like Seekers, each one different, but cut from a common lump of clay. The pattern on the cup, plates and bowl, speaks of God as our Source and our Caller from the Deeps of Creation with its pattern of waves and circles."

Stalking the Spirit

Over time, both chalice and plate have been broken and mended, reminding us that we are, indeed, a fragile earthen vessel.

INCLUDING CHILDREN

From the beginning, Seekers made an earnest search for meaningful ways to include our children in both the inward journey of prayer and self-reflection and the outward journey of mission in the city. While Fred and

Sonya were reworking the call of Seekers, Fred attended a class reunion at Yale Divinity School and ran across a book by John Westerhoff, a professor at Duke Divinity School, titled *Will Our Children Have Faith?* Fred came back excited by what he saw and the two of them circulated an article by Westerhoff on children's learning through liturgy.

Fred and Sonya invited a young father, Dave Lloyd, to join them on a visit to Westerhoff at Duke. That visit gave a blessing to the direction they were taking at Seekers. John Westerhoff affirmed the intimacy of a small community that would include elders for memory, middle-aged people for vision, and children for a sense of reality. He urged them to include children in the full life of the community as the primary way that they would "catch" the faith of other adults besides their parents. Westerhoff also validated the importance of training everyone for membership through the School of Christian Living and mission groups. He spoke at length about the importance of liturgy and worship, and expressed some concern about the loyalty that people might develop for one's mission group rather than the whole community.

Seekers embraced their identity within Church of the Saviour as "the children's church," and struggled to find ways of learning from children rather than dumbing down worship for them. Efforts at inclusion focused on pre-worship community-building activities: celebrating birthdays and honors at school, announcements of inclusive activities, and practicing songs for worship. Now known as "circle time," we understand this pre-worship gathering time as a chance to connect as an intergenerational community, to share personal news, and to keep each other informed of movies, meetings, and other events. Visitors sometimes feel they have stumbled into a family gathering before worship, but this gathering time helps everyone to straggle in and settle down before worship begins.

DECISION-MAKING

In Church of the Saviour, core members focused on their weekly mission groups and let the church staff handle questions of vision, direction, and financial oversight. C of S members rarely gathered for a congregational meeting, and then only to make decisions about polity or property. Years could pass without such a meeting. Their basic loyalty and decision-making power lay in the mission groups, to which only members or intern members (people on the path toward membership) could belong. Regular attenders were not considered members at C of S.

In Seekers, all core members were expected to participate in monthly meetings for policy discussions, budget matters, and care for the whole community. Sonya felt it was a way for core members to share power and develop their identification with Seekers. For the first decade, monthly meetings were held in each other's homes as a conscious effort to include personal connections in the process of forming community. Meetings lasted three hours or more, including a potluck meal. Different people took leadership for worship, moderating the meeting, taking notes, and facilitating different items on the agenda. Fred and Sonya were treated as peers in the circle of core members, bound by the same commitments all had made, even though they were being paid a stipend as part-time co-pastors.

To encourage more engagement with the broader issues facing Seekers, Sonya circulated these questions for discussion at several core group meetings:

1. Mission: How can we encourage sharing and ownership of a mission whether we participate directly or not?
2. Evangelism: Until now, we've tried to attract unaffiliated CoS members. Now it's time to look beyond CoS, asking who Christ might be calling us to witness to and invite to Seekers.
3. Education: Assuming that everything we do as church has the potential of being a vehicle for Christian education, how can we better address the needs of children and adults? Is our pre-worship time serving that function?
4. Financial Stewardship: How can we more consciously take on responsibility for being good stewards of our money?
5. Worship: Where do we stand now on the issue of continuity vs. diversity of leadership? What images, symbols and rituals are taking root among us which help shape our identity?
6. Ecumenical Ties: What gifts do we have to offer the larger CoS family and they to us? What kind of linkages would be mutually helpful?

Those questions would continue to circulate periodically during the first decade of Seekers' life together, inviting the core group to assume leadership in all those areas.

FIRST MISSION GROUP

Formation of the Artists' Group presented core members with the opportunity to think about how new mission groups would be approved in Seekers. Liz Vail and Mary Clare Powell had been together in a C of S mission group called The Alabaster Jar, but when C of S split up that group ended. Now, as founding members of Seekers, Liz and Mary Clare wrote out their call for the Artists' Group and circulated it among potential members. When three others responded, the first new mission group at Seekers was born. Liz and Mary Clare linked the group with the circle of core members, establishing at Seekers the C of S pattern of having at least two core members in each mission group for coordination and accountability.

The Artists' Group was called to support each person in a different form of expression, but not to pursue a single corporate mission—the primary issue of Seekers' acceptability within the wider church. Another facet was the importance of art and creativity at Seekers, rather than mitigating the plight of the poor. From the beginning, Seekers attracted artists because of its emphasis on creative expression, both visual and written. Years later, Sonya made a strong case for *art* and *advocacy* as the primary charisms of Seekers. Formation of the Artists' Group was the first step toward claiming that identity.

As rituals for joining, including children in Communion, and formation of a mission group were taking place in Seekers, a sharp debate emerged in the new C of S council. Now that the sister churches were beginning to function with separate budgets and different worship centers, there was some question about the function and financial support of the C of S staff. Gordon suggested to the council that the corporate call of Church of the Saviour could be expressed in terms of their staff functions. According to our council representative, Gordon saw himself as the visionary pastor-prophet, Bill Branner as financial manager, and Elizabeth O'Connor as the spiritual director, and he saw Church of the Saviour continuing much as it had before.

The council took no position on Gordon's description how the C of S staff would function, but they did decide that *any new member of Church of the Saviour would have to join one of the sister churches, not the parent church*. In effect, the C of S staff was released to focus on new missions, while the new churches became responsible for previously established missions, and also for ongoing spiritual formation of their members through mission groups.

Seekers wanted more visibility for the new churches. We suggested that every month one of the sister communities should lead worship for the ecumenical service so everyone would have a chance to experience the nature of their worship directly, but the council refused to interfere with the pattern of Gordon's preaching at the second service in the sanctuary at 2025. When the question arose about what standard would be applied when admitting a new church to the C of S council, the Seekers representative on the council declined to vote in favor of a proposal that *corporate mission* be the guideline, saying that she needed to discuss it first with Seekers. She was afraid that if a single corporate mission for each church became the standard, Seekers would not meet that qualification.

These questions took on more edge in the fall of 1977 because, for the first time, each community was permitted to write its own commitment statement for core members. Seekers decided to retain the C of S statement for another year because there were other things to worry about, and they wanted to indicate solidarity even as they were developing a separate identity.

PATH TO MEMBERSHIP

With such a broad understanding of call to ministry in daily life at Seekers, the question was how to hold it together. Since nobody was being paid for full-time leadership, the members' commitment statement was the only constant that everyone relied upon, so defining membership became the focus of discussion.

There was much discomfort among Seekers about Church of the Saviour's distinction between members and non-members. In the C of S tradition, membership required at least two years of preparation in the School of Christian Living, a promise to tithe one's income, daily prayer and study, and participation in a mission group. Intern members of C of S could join a mission group by declaring themselves on the path to membership, but regular attenders could not even belong to a mission group.

Nobody at Seekers wanted to water down the strong commitment of the core group, but the implication that loyal attenders were "non-members" rankled. Newcomers at Seekers wanted to join mission groups and be involved in the decision-making process more quickly, so core members decided that anyone who wanted to join a mission group could do so after taking any two classes in the School. They did not need to declare themselves as intern members, and they might not ever become core members. Seekers felt that commitment to the call and disciplines of a mission group was enough for some, although they hoped a few new people would be called to the more demanding work of core membership each year.

For those who felt called to become committed members at Seekers, the core group reduced the number of required courses in the School from five to three twelve-week courses (Hebrew Testament, New Testament, and Spiritual Growth). Core members also affirmed individual spiritual practices for ongoing personal formation. Those disciplines included daily "quiet time" for prayer, study and reflection, weekly worship, a written spiritual report (if in a mission group) or accountability relationship, tithing one's income to Seekers, a yearly silent retreat, and intentional yearly recommitment.

Sonya believed that everyone should be invited to join the body of Seekers when they felt ready to make a commitment to Christ and to intentional spiritual growth in this particular community. She drafted a general commitment statement in 1978, but I found no evidence that she asked for approval by core members. Her draft reflected her desire for more inclusion:

> I will seek to bring every phase of my life under the Lordship of Christ. As a member of the Seekers Community, I pledge myself to live out this commitment:
>
> - by seeking to learn what it means to be church in the world today;
> - by intentionally including all facets of my life in this ongoing process; and
> - by being flexible and willing to embrace the new and the creative in our own midst and in the world.
>
> When I move from this place I will join some other expression of the Christian Church.

Sonya's statement would have allowed people to join Seekers without belonging to a mission group, but the other committed members were apparently not ready for that. Instead of opening membership to everyone, Seekers generally shifted their language to identify everyone as a member, and those who made a public commitment as *core members*.

By the end of 1978, stalking the Spirit in our daily lives had become a widely shared endeavor at Seekers. Core members were exercising more responsibility for worship and education, for starting new mission groups, and for inviting other members of the community toward fuller participation and accountability. The Tuesday night School of Christian Living, although still under the aegis of Church of the Saviour, was full of Seekers who were giving and taking classes. It was a place to practice leading and following, creativity and community. In worship and at the school, shared leadership had clearly taken root in Seekers.

4

Spiritual Formation in Community
Worship, Retreats, and Mission Groups

WORSHIP WAS THE OBVIOUS place to nurture the whole community because it was the one place where we gathered and could know ourselves as a single body of Christ. Fred worked hard to make his sermons a challenge to stretch and grow. Sonya rarely preached, but as the regular liturgist her careful attention to language and symbolism invited the interweaving of personal story, our communal story, and God's creation story. Together they sought to deepen our roots in the Spirit, and trust that God was at work in and through our daily lives.

In her role as the worship leader, Sonya's attention to language and silence moved us away from our self-centered concerns toward the possibility of new life in Christ. Instead of a focus on the pain and suffering of Jesus, Seekers heard more language of empowerment and nurture by the Spirit. Here is an example of Sonya's prayer language from her collection of prayers, *Growing Our Life Together*, which is available on the Seekers website.

> Gracious creator, spirit of prophetic wisdom,
> your seed is planted in our soul.
>
> Together we are creating and seeking to embody
> your vision for life.
>
> Empower our awareness of you that it may
> nurture and enable us
> to offer who we are becoming.

> May all the elements and creatures of the universe
> be known as sacred and be honored as your holy creation.

Hearing this kind of language as we opened ourselves to *divine oneness* during worship enlarged our understanding of the mysterious work of the Spirit. Over time, the liturgy in Seekers worship became the primary place to deepen our inner journey together, as well as broadening the range of outward concerns for social justice.

FIRST OVERNIGHT: A NOT-SILENT RETREAT

In addition to worship, Sonya looked for other ways to nurture the whole community through work and play together. She wanted our spiritual life to be fun and exciting as well as challenging. All Seekers were invited to the first overnight, using the new Wellspring cabins to give everyone a bed. "We are so often together working to solve an issue or finish a task," the invitation said, "that we seldom have enough time just to be with each other in an unplanned, fun, spontaneous way." The cost for individuals and families was heavily subsidized in order to encourage participation. Most of the community came.

After the success of that first overnight, these community gatherings were offered twice a year at Wellspring. Typically, about sixty people came—half of them children! Overnights provided unstructured time to play outdoors with the children and to make art and sing corny camp songs together. In the fall, apple picking turned into applesauce making, and when it was close to Halloween, pumpkin carving sometimes turned competitive. In the spring, we were more inclined to listen for frogs and watch for fawns feeding in the gauzy dawn. For young families, the overnights were a safe place for children to "run wild" together. For those without children, the sleepovers often felt chaotic, but important for the whole community to discover other ways of connecting.

Also on the Dayspring property, but in a different location, silent retreats were scheduled for Seekers twice a year. Since Dayspring Retreat could house only eighteen people, and core members were committed to attending one silent retreat each year, they went most regularly. Usually someone from Seekers led those retreats, offering minimal direction and lots of space to be fed directly by the silence, the land, and the seasons, reminding us that we are part of the larger creation story. While not obvious to a casual visitor, silent retreats deepened our spiritual life together, and they sharpened a sense of the Spirit being at the heart of Seekers. By letting go of our verbal skills, we often discovered a pool of love and care to draw from when differences arose among the core members.

A MISSION FOR SEEKERS?

In 1978, Fred announced that he had been invited to visit an interracial church in South Africa, and because of his work with FLOC he was particularly interested in going. Apartheid was then the law in South Africa, and Fred was intrigued by the different model that Trevor Hudson's Methodist church was attempting to create. There was some discussion of the sexism involved in supporting Fred's trip to South Africa while Sonya stayed behind, but his absence was approved and money was set aside for his ticket.

Sonya shared a remarkably frank letter to the core group that illustrates the courage and vibrancy she brought to their partnership. Specifically, Sonya asked "How is this mission for Seekers?" and "How should the gap left by Fred's absence be filled?" There was no immediate answer to her first question, although it was clear that some relationship with a mission in South Africa might develop out of Fred's visit. Sonya wanted missions that were closer to home.

Disappointment over Sonya's role as the "keeper of the homefires" continued to fuel conversations about gender expectations among Seekers, so a women's theology group formed to read and discuss these issues. Although not widely publicized, the group gave some key women a place to discuss the rich diet of feminist theology that was being published in the late seventies, amid the contentious debates over women's ordination in mainline denominations and the passage of the Equal Rights Amendment in the political arena.

Fred asked Liz Vail to make a banner for him to take from Seekers to South Africa. As an artist and painter, Liz proceeded by claiming her "authority at the point of gift." Elizabeth O'Connor had used that term in her book *The Eighth Day of Creation*, where she wrote, "Our obedience and surrender to God are in large part our obedience and surrender to our gifts." At C of S, that meant each person might claim some kind of leadership where their particular gifts were offered for the work and well-being of the whole. For Liz, it meant that others would participate but also recognize her authority to hold the vision for the whole project.

As a member of the Artists' Group, Liz trusted the power of attraction, and she relied on that spirit for inspiration and guidance. This kind of tutelage was described in O'Connor's book as being a "patron of gifts," but Liz put herself in a Seekerly stance of co-learner and co-seer. Liz claimed her authority as the convening artist, but she allowed the form to take shape around the gifts of other people. For her, it was a deliberate act of stalking the Spirit. When it was finished, the three-sided burlap column, studded with ceramic beads and unspun wool, spoke to her of the Trinity "over against the current culture."

More than any other single event at Seekers that year, Liz Vail's banner gave visibility to the spiritual life and working theology of Seekers. It was definitely an experience of shared leadership in process. Of course, not everyone saw Liz's banner as a thing of beauty. Some wondered if this gift of process could be fully appreciated in South Africa. Nevertheless, Fred folded it up and took it with him, publically acknowledging Liz's authority at the point of her gift.

From South Africa that summer, Fred wrote to the Dyers about wanting to help resettle some of the people he had met who had been targeted by the white South African government for their activism against apartheid. For Sonya, resettling refugees from South Africa was not a primary goal for Seekers. In a note to herself dated September 1978, Sonya listed her primary concerns for Seekers under the heading "needs to be answered." She wanted to develop relationships with those who were just beginning to connect with Seekers, continue deepening the spiritual life within the body of believers, and raise our consciousness about needs in the wider world without getting mired in a single mission. She did not want to be distracted with a far-off mission in South Africa.

In spite of Sonya's reluctance, Fred invited Trevor Hudson, the Methodist pastor he had visited in South Africa, for an exchange visit to Seekers. Hudson came the next year, along with a black South African pastor and his wife. Their visit exposed us directly to the political situation in South Africa and the HIV/Aids health crisis there. It particularly touched Paul Holmes, a Seeker who was then working for USAID. On his next trip to South Africa, Paul visited a health clinic in Winterveldt, a desolate "reservation" near Pretoria, and he began to make yearly requests for financial aid to support the clinic. However, helping at-risk youth in Winterveldt did not become a real mission for Seekers until much later.

Spiritual Formation in Community

After Hudson's visit, there was more criticism at the monthly members meeting about Fred's preaching, and he confessed to feeling hurt by the suggestions that he be more relational in the pulpit. Fred later said that he felt he had become the target for feelings of loss, fears of the future, and some of the paternal projections that Gordon carried in Church of the Saviour. Because worship was at the heart of Seekers' call to be church, it was the place where people were most aware of missing Gordon's visionary preaching. Fred's trip to South Africa may also have sharpened the mood of critique, since during his absence other people from the community were preaching, allowing us to experience a variety of preaching styles.

MISSION SUPPORT GROUP

The second mission group to form within Seekers was the Mission Support Group (MSG). Fred and Sonya saw MSG as a natural extension of Seekers' call to support ministry in daily life, and Fred became a founding member. It met every other week and did not have a common task other than to support those who saw their work as mission. As a studio potter searching for what my ministry might be, I joined MSG when it formed. Both the Artists' Group and MSG met every other week, and because they did not ask people to be involved in a shared task, neither group really challenged people to grow in loving others unlike themselves. Instead, both groups reinforced the practice of individual calls being supported by Seekers.

Peter and I were the first couple to arrive at Seekers without prior membership in Church of the Saviour. People were suspicious that we would "use" the community and then move away because of Peter's military career, but generally we were welcomed and given many opportunities to offer our gifts and prior experience with small groups. We had been exposed to C of S through *Faith at Work* magazine and The Ram's Horn, a coffeehouse in Hanover that was patterned after The Potter's House, so we stepped into Seekers' culture of commitment with some experience from afar. Others, informed by Elizabeth O'Connor's books, were likewise drawn to explore Church of the Saviour in its new form of belonging through the six sister churches.

Couples were encouraged not to join the same mission group within C of S, so that each person could focus on one's call to a particular place of service, and in order to avoid the conventional pattern of couples serving on a committee together. Seekers continued that practice in order to encourage independent spiritual formation for all members of a mission group. Thus, once he had completed two classes in the School, Peter joined the Tuesday night Shepherds mission group just before it became part of Seekers.

LEARNERS & TEACHERS

Church of the Saviour had always emphasized continuing education School of Christian Living (SCL) for all members. When the New Lands process gave birth to six new churches, the council decided to continue the SCL as a C of S mission so that those churches would not have to organize separate schools. However, by 1979 the Tuesday night Shepherds group was made up entirely of Seekers, and students from the wider C of S community clustered around the Thursday night school because that was where Gordon, Mary, and Elizabeth O'Connor could be found.

Since most of the Tuesday night classes were also being taught by Seekers, it felt like the right time to claim Tuesday night for a Seekers SCL at 2025. Emily Benson circulated the call for a new mission group in Seekers, which would be called Learners and Teachers (L&T). The purpose of L&T would be "to provide educational opportunities that promote wholeness of the individual and society."

Registration for the first session was slow because David Lloyd's New Testament class was in direct competition with Mary Cosby's New Testament class on Thursday night, but by the winter term in 1980, L&T announced a full schedule of three classes for Seekers' SCL, each one filled with six to twelve participants. The school began with dinner prepared by a couple of the participants, a short meditation to focus on the spiritual component of our gathering, and then separation into different ninety-minute classes. Participants were expected to read and prepare a written assignment each week, and they frequently had a prayer partner from the class to contact for conversation between class sessions.

L&T worked hard to make sure that those who were teaching classes were capable of building relational community as well as offering good content for students. Over time, a pattern of offerings developed. Each term of the school would feature a biblical class, a mission or spiritual growth class, and a "fun" class (like clowning or liturgical dance). The L&T mission group had full authority at the point of its call to decide which classes to offer and who would teach them. The school frequently attracted participants from other churches with no adult education program, and core members were encouraged to attend classes to encourage newcomers into our culture of shared leadership. The school was seen as an essential part of nurturing the whole community with ongoing study and opportunities for deepening our relationships with one another, as well as preparing people for core membership at Seekers.

CELEBRATION CIRCLE

In the fall of 1979, another key mission group formed at Seekers. Celebration Circle (CC) would "work to create new kinds of worship experiences" and support the worship life of Seekers by "giving energy to our community celebrations of God's presence in our lives." Sonya was a founding member of CC, and her enthusiasm for creative worship was a driving force for the group. The work of CC consisted of the practical, week-to-week tasks of preparing liturgies for Sunday worship, coordinating music, and creating altars and bulletins. Inviting a mission group to design worship required openness to many different preferences: silence vs. group sharing, short and long sermons, folk songs, praise music, traditional hymns, recorded classical music, dance, and drama. All those possibilities were hashed out in the weekly mission group meetings. Peter moved to Celebration Circle when it formed, and I left MSG to join Learners & Teachers because of my interest in ongoing adult education as the essential ingredient for shared leadership. Although Fred still decided who would be preaching each week, he stayed with MSG and did not join Celebration Circle.

By 1980, a critical framework of four mission groups had taken shape within Seekers, like the boney skeleton of this body of Christ. In each mission group, the moderator and spiritual director held the combined purpose of inward reflection and outward action. At first only core members held those key positions, but later they were selected from within the group and might not be core members. Unlike Church of the Saviour, Seekers never restricted mission group membership to core members. After completing two classes in the School, anyone was free to explore with a mission group to test for a mutual sense of rightness. Each week, mission group members were expected to write a short spiritual report, which allowed for an intimate and prayerful conversation with the spiritual director of the group.

Within Seekers, mission groups became the primary place for belonging, and for confession and forgiveness, so that people could come to worship ready to celebrate God's presence in the world. Commitment to the call of the group held each group together, while differences of temperament and skill could be worked out, gifts named, and roles identified, so each person had a specific way to contribute.

Not all natural groupings became mission groups. Through a class in liturgical clowning, several people wanted to bring more drama and dance to worship, and the class was given permission by Celebration Circle to perform the gospel lesson each week during Advent. Because clowning drew many people who were already anchored in other mission groups, the "Faith & Fantasy" group never did become a mission group. Instead, the clowns met whenever there was a reason to design an event. Members went to children's hospital and retirement homes, did clown skits for Seekers worship, and went to other churches to offer weekend workshops, which often brought new people to the Seekers School of Christian Living on Tuesday nights. Over the next decade, Faith & Fantasy provided a regular schedule of clown classes in the SCL and invited a whole generation of Seekers toward embodying what St. Paul called "the foolishness of Christ."

FRICTION WITH STAFF

In June of 1979, friction developed between Seekers and the C of S staff once again. This time Elizabeth O'Connor explained to Sonya that there were "too many copies" of the booklet, which had been published after the New Lands, to consider redoing it if Seekers were to change the language of their membership commitment. At the same time, the 2025 users committee wrangled about the five parking spaces behind the church during the week and finally assigned one to Fred because of his FLOC office there, but there was no space for Sonya. She was the "new kid on the block" and was having a hard time establishing her place there as Fred's partner.

Seekers then received a letter from Elizabeth posing a series of questions she wanted to use for a book on where the New Lands process was taking the church. The questionnaire conveyed Elizabeth's concerns about the "integrity of membership" as it was being practiced in the sister communities. Seekers held several meetings at which all members of the community were invited to reflect on those questions. That participatory method of engaging with questions simply would not have happened in the parent church, but it was Sonya's way of stimulating broader involvement.

Spiritual Formation in Community

In Seekers, there was a growing desire to include everyone when the result would impact the whole community.

Seekers sent their response to O'Connor's questionnaire along with attachments that described our call to be church instead of being defined by mission. In answer to Elizabeth's question "What have been or are the places of hardship for your community?" Seekers responded forthrightly: "The places of hardship for our community have focused around tensions with the ecumenical staff and church council. These have led to feelings of not being included and valued for our diversity in the same way others have been valued for their similarity."

Elizabeth's inquiry about desired changes brought a long list from Seekers in keeping with our call to shared leadership. The vision for Seekers which they submitted reveals how important the critique of gender roles had become in Seekers:

> Continued growth in exploring individual ministries and combining them as new calls emerge; continued desire not to settle into "middle-class thinking"; continued evoking of diverse gifts; continued grappling with issues of Christian relevance to all of life: males and females working together as equals, the masculine/feminine within each of us, sharing leadership in differing ways (i.e., no one being stereotyped as a particular kind of leader whether it be a teacher or dinner-preparer).

The language of Seekers' reply may sound quarrelsome and dated, but the issues were lively and relevant then. As mainline denominations battled over ordination for women, many of the women at Seekers mobilized to support the Equal Rights Amendment. Although the ERA was never adopted as a constitutional amendment, the political effort raised awareness of gender inequities everywhere. Fred reported that his own relationship with the C of S staff was friendly and collegial during this period. "But," he said, "I think Sonya felt shut out of her dream to be accepted as an equal." Whether Sonya's dream was realistic or not, it shaped Seekers in those early years.

Many of the newer women who were attracted to Seekers did identify with Sonya's aspirations because we were facing similar struggles in the workplace. Sonya represented women who wanted to be treated as equals within male-dominated systems, even when they did not have the experience or explicit credentials. For many, Sonya's natural gifts for listening deeply and encouraging a more distributed model of leadership seemed more important than Fred's academic preparation or Gordon's singular style.

LETTERS TO THE SCATTERED CHURCHES

Periodically throughout 1978 and 1979, Elizabeth O'Connor circulated what she called "Letters to the Scattered Pilgrims." Initially they appeared as separate undated missives of common concern, and they provide an outline of issues that C of S staff thought were important. By the end of 1979, they were published as another book from Church of the Saviour, titled *Letters to Scattered Pilgrims*.

Although Elizabeth featured each of the other communities in one of these letters, Seekers was barely mentioned. Instead, her last letter was titled, "On Children in the Wilderness," in which she described the FLOC Wilderness School. Although many Seekers were involved with various FLOC mission groups, and Fred was still the FLOC director, Seekers had refused to claim FLOC as our corporate mission. The publication of the book of letters left Seekers feeling invisible and marginalized from the C of S community, because so few of the issues raised by Seekers in response to her questionnaire had been addressed in the book or with the C of S council.

The following year, Gordon circulated his self-assessment to members of the C of S council. His view of the New Lands process was quite different from the understanding that Seekers held. He said to the council:

> Wellspring and the Church of the Saviour support staff are complementary in their ministry to the World Church.... We are inundated with requests to share who we are.... Betty O's books—seven, all in print—perhaps nurture in depth more people than any contemporary religious author. Her writing grows out of the whole CoS community.... There need be no attempt to equalize what each faith community draws from the resources (facilities, staff, etc.) of the whole.

With that, Gordon put the council on notice that he would continue to speak as though Church of the Saviour was a single entity, and that he was willing to help new missions wherever they might develop but had no intention of guiding the whole enterprise. Instead, his call was to "share who we are" with the world church. Since the council refused to be a place for dialogue, the question of who would represent Church of the Saviour to the wider world remained unanswered as each community struggled to find its identity within the C of S family.

Then, in 1980, the council asked World Peacemakers, a mission group directly associated with the C of S but not one of the sister churches, *not* to speak as Church of the Saviour. It was the first time that one of the independent mission groups had been chastened by the council. As a result, the second-generation churches also agreed *not* to represent themselves as Church of the Saviour. Furthermore, they agreed that the sister churches would use the wording "in the tradition of Church of the Saviour" instead of identifying themselves as a C of S community. By subtraction, then, only the C of S staff and Wellspring, a C of S mission group located at the Dayspring Farm, would speak as Church of the Saviour.

INFORMAL CONNECTIONS

Meanwhile, the normal joys and sorrows of life continued to create bonds among Seekers. When Muriel and Ed Lipp's son committed suicide, the whole community mourned with them. More than anyone else at Seekers, Muriel carried a deep loyalty to Church of the Saviour along with her devotion to Seekers. Fred Taylor and Gordon Cosby conducted Eddie's memorial service at 2025 together, and the wider C of S community gathered around the Lipp family in their grief. Perhaps it was also a time to mourn the loss of the original church.

A year later, Muriel and Ed's daughter, who had grown up in C of S, was married at 2025. That day, the old brownstone mansion provided an elegant setting, full of flowers, good food, and warm friendship—an extended family reunion after the hard years of developing separate communities.

There were plenty of more informal celebrations at Seekers. Each week during circle time, the gathered body would sing our own version of "Happy Birthday" to any eligible child or adult. Those occasions usually resulted in extra refreshments, balloons, and general hilarity during the coffee hour, which happened upstairs after worship. If the clowns had been part of worship on that day, red dots (signs of the Holy Spirit) would make everyone's face part of the surprise. Personal friendships, shared vacations, dance parties, and periodic canoe trips also enriched the growing sense of community beyond planned meeting times and formal structures.

Desire for discussion and fellowship, without the overlay of policy and commitment, sparked another ongoing group, the "Second Wave," in the early eighties. Hollis Vail had retired from the Defense Mapping Agency and joined Seekers through his marriage to Liz. Jane Lieper had been a missionary in China, was widowed early, raised four children on her own, and had worked for the National Council of Churches. Both felt a desire for more intentional fellowship among those who were not in mission groups, and so they "put out a call" to see who else might be interested.

About fifteen people responded to their invitation and Second Wave met monthly for the next five years or so, functioning as a supportive circle around the core members. Jane urged Second Wave to sponsor a gala Christmas potluck before the evening service on Christmas Eve, so the group pitched in with linens, flowers, and candles on every table. The dining room, sanctuary, and second floor of 2025 were packed with Seekers before a simple service of lessons and carols. The following Easter, Jane again led Second Wave to host a joyfully decorated Easter morning breakfast before worship. Flowers, candles, and Easter eggs made each table a festive sight, and the old square piano fairly groaned with good food.

After that, Christmas dinner and Easter breakfast became yearly traditions for Seekers. As children grew up and went off to college, and people moved to different neighborhoods around Washington, DC, Christmas and Easter gatherings became a way to reconnect from far-flung places in the world. Now people often bring visiting family members as well, so the tables at these gatherings are alive with new faces and old friends.

5

Money as a Working Theology
"Where Your Treasure Is . . ."

WHILE MANY CHURCHES SHY away from talk of money as a spiritual matter, Seekers worked hard to create a culture of transparency and accountability. Practicing generosity and financial accountability were major themes at Seekers from the beginning. Since all of the original core members came out of Church of the Saviour, their understanding of the membership commitment was to "proportional giving, beginning with a tithe of one's gross income."

Both Sonya and Fred raised the issue of college expenses for families with children as they drew up the call of Seekers. They believed that family life was valid ministry and they also recognized that financial resources were often a point of tension between men and women because of their unequal earning power and childcare responsibilities, so they saw the expectation of tithing as a justice issue as well. At Seekers, the giving expectation for core members pertained simply to income, rather than specifying gross income. That gave core members more flexibility for figuring the basis for their tithe at Seekers.

ZERO-BASE BUDGET

Within the first year of Seekers' existence, core members adopted a policy of "zero-base budgeting," which meant that they would not seek to build a reserve fund to carry over from year to year. Based on the biblical story of gathering manna for each day, the first members agreed that Seekers would focus on God's generosity and abundance, and not store up funds for a "rainy day." Of course, that was more possible because we used space at 2025 and did not own a building, which would require maintenance. Although we set aside money for our use of 2025, Seekers paid Fred and Sonya an equal amount for whatever time they spent on Seekers and planned to give away an equal amount for outreach.

When the Church of the Saviour council decided that any bequests that came to C of S would be divided equally among the sister communities, Seekers agreed that our share should be invested in existing structures for social good rather than being spent immediately on C of S missions. Once Manna emerged from Jubilee Church to purchase distressed properties, upgrade them, and sell them to low-income residents of the city, Seekers put all subsequent bequests into the Manna Capstone Fund as a loan. It was a way to meet our guidelines for bequests and also support a ministry that we believed in.

At the new Wellspring conference center, on the Dayspring property, Don McClanen began a ministry to explore the spiritual issues of money more systematically. Fred was an eager participant in this "Ministry of Money" because FLOC was so involved with the consequences of poverty, and he was trying to help families become more stable. The initial study group pondered scriptures on money and probed family attitudes about security, and each participant worked on a financial inventory to address the vagueness that often hid debts or resources they didn't want to count. Afterward, Fred preached about his experience at Wellspring, and there was a class on money in the School of Christian Living.

In Elizabeth O'Connor's book *Letters to the Scattered Pilgrims*, two chapters focused on money as a spiritual issue. She quoted Gordon on our human need to give, and how the poor as well as the rich have a need to give: "To give away money," he said, "is to win a victory over the dark powers that oppress us."

Seekers approached giving as an act of gratitude rather than a struggle with "dark powers." Fred and Sonya emphasized giving through Seekers as an act of commitment to the community, and they encouraged our outreach giving to be guided by active participation. It was an invitation to become advocates for the service organizations where we were already giving our time.

As we began to engage the issues of power and gender roles associated with money, Sonya and Fred encouraged each of the core members to write

Money as a Working Theology

a money autobiography as background for our discussions. I have included the autobiography questions because O'Connor's book is out of print:

Money Autobiography Questions

1. What is your happiest memory in connection with money? Your unhappiest?
2. What role did money have in your childhood? Your mother's attitude? Your father's attitude? Did you feel poor? Rich? Did you worry about money?
3. What was your attitude toward money as a teenager? Your memories from this period about money?
4. What role did money play in your life as a young adult? As a parent? At age 47? 54? 61? 68? Did your attitude shift at different ages? What is your attitude now?
5. What is your present financial status? Your monthly income? Other assets? Will you inherit money?
6. What do you consider responsible financial planning for the future?
7. Do you see yourself as generous? Stingy? Do you know how much money you have? Do you take risks with money? Do you worry about money? Be specific.
8. Are there other issues connected with money that you worry about?

As Seekers embraced the discussion of personal values and choices about giving from current income or total wealth, responsibility for maintaining the property and buildings at Dayspring Farm raised ongoing questions within Church of the Saviour. Just then, Dayspring Church was requesting additional contributions from each community for maintenance of the farm properties. Since the sister churches actually owned the Dayspring property together, Seekers felt it should be covered by the C of S budget. Questions were raised among core members at Seekers about the lack of relationship between Dayspring Church and the Wellspring mission group, which was still affiliated directly with C of S. By then, Seekers had begun to identify themselves as creating a new vision for being church "in the tradition of Church of the Saviour," and they saw Wellspring as promoting a vision of C of S that no longer existed because of the New Lands process, but attempts to raise this issue with other council members went nowhere.

GROWING EDGE FUND

Sonya asked for financial help to attend the world conference in Copenhagen to launch the United Nations "Decade for Women" in 1980. It would mean two and a half weeks away, a first for Sonya since Seekers formed. Members agreed that it would balance their support for Fred's previous trip to South Africa, and Liz Vail offered to be Sonya's "partner" for the trip, raising her name up in prayer and acting as a spiritual friend in preparation and follow-up. This kind of *intentional partnering* became a model at Seekers.

Liz identified creativity as a charism of Seekers because of our call to ministry in daily life. Recalling her rich experience of creating a banner for Fred to take with him to South Africa, she asked, "Could the church be a patron of the arts in a generative way?" In answer to that question, Liz and Hollis Vail gave $1,000 to start the Growing Edge Fund to encourage calls that might be emerging in Seekers. They said that "seed money generates interaction, raises consciousness, builds community, and energizes both the individual and the community." They specifically wanted to encourage potential that was undeveloped, rather than furthering a known skill or interest. They wanted Growing Edge money to be available to any member of the community (not just core members), to be used for a new venture in faith, and to involve partnership with someone else in the community for support and accountability.

The first Growing Edge grantee was Mary Clare Powell, who wanted to self-publish a book about her mother, Ruth. The book project was a new venture for Mary Clare, combining her skill as a professional writer with her creative longing to be a photographer. Released in 1981, her book, *The Widow*, was truly a work of art and heart. It was a realistic portrait of her mother, a woman of very modest means who was living richly and consciously into old age. It was the first of many books to emerge from this creative congregation.[1]

The next year, Mary Clare and her partner left on a two-year cross-country road trip, photographing art and interviewing women for a much larger research project. From their trip, a book was published in 1985: *This Way Daybreak Comes: Women's Values and the Future*. Many copies were sold at Seekers, and the book was also carried at The Potter's House. Although Mary Clare left Seekers to undertake a PhD at the University

---

1. Appendix 8.

of Massachusetts, she returned to lead our first women's retreat in 1986. In subsequent years she has also presented several books of poetry at The Potter's House.

Not all Growing Edge requests were approved, even when the fund had not been depleted for that year. Liz wrote in her Growing Edge diary that "facing no is as important as saying yes in the creative process." Within a couple of years, the Growing Edge Fund had been adopted as a line item in the Seekers budget, and the amount was raised to $3,000. Over the next few years, Growing Edge grants helped people attend the Lay Ministry Lab, go to the Christ in the Desert Monastery in New Mexico, attend a national clown training event, purchase a lathe for a new woodworker, and help another capitalize a new graphics business.

As a way for the church to support new calls that need to be tested by members of the congregation, the Growing Edge Fund has been a source of microenterprise funding and spiritual companionship for such possibilities. Although the amount of money given to any single grantee has not been large, the fund has encouraged many new ventures. It has allowed some people to discover a definitive "no" as well.

GENDER AND MONEY ISSUES

During the pastoral decade (1976–87), guidance from Fred and Sonya about financial giving set the direction for Seekers. Since most people at Seekers worked at government jobs or non-profits, there did not seem to be any great wealth in the community. Younger families wrestled with the expectation for tithing out of current income and core members discussed what base they ought to use for tithing at Seekers. Did tithing mean 10 percent of gross income, current salary, or net income after expenses? What about those with no income of their own? Some questioned the idea of tithing altogether.

The issue of gender and power in relation to money came up in 1981 when David Lloyd decided to leave core membership and his wife, Sharon, joined the core group instead. By then, they had two little girls, and the commitment to tithe on his gross income was more of a burden for David than what was expected of someone like Emily or Muriel, since neither of their spouses were involved at Seekers. The pay differential between men and women affected other young families as well, making money a barrier to membership for several men. Although he was not a core member,

David remained interested and engaged, especially toward issues of money and stewardship at Seekers.

Fred urged that we look at tithing prophetically, asking "What do we believe about money?" He suggested that we focus on this as a subject for worship, study, and dialogue. Answers were not quick to develop, but the questions surfaced in many conversations. Since then, the questions about tithing—what basis to use and how couples might work with those issues—have resurfaced periodically, which has refreshed the culture of generosity at Seekers and encouraged people to make new choices about money. We were, in fact, wrestling with the dark powers of money. Giving was one way to engage the power of our consumer culture.

It took five years for core members to finally settle the question of pay equity for Fred and Sonya. By then, members were no longer willing to peg Fred's salary to what he was getting from FLOC, which also freed them to affirm the gifts that Sonya brought, even though she did not have his level of formal theological education. As they considered a different standard, core members agreed that they wanted to offer Fred and Sonya (counted together) the salary of a single full-time church leader with skills to lead a non-profit agency—someone who would draw a yearly salary of $20,000 at that time. Since Sonya was working three days a week for Seekers and Fred claimed two days a week, her stipend was raised to $12,000 and he was paid $8,000. This was the first time they were paid different amounts.

In 1981 and 1982, core membership dropped to eleven, down from the nineteen who founded Seekers. Given the financial backbone that the disciplines of membership provided for Seekers (about 75 percent of the contributed income), there was real concern about meeting the budget. Instead of worry, however, the image of pruning and repotting Seekers in fresh soil threaded through budget discussions. There was a general feeling of hopefulness about the new people who were coming toward Seekers, so the budget was not reduced. Instead of fear, a sense of trust and optimism prevailed.

When notified that FLOC would be moving out of the headquarters building at 2025, core members were eager to use the additional space, and they discussed whether Seekers should offer to pay more for greater use of the building. However, when Gordon set a price per square foot for additional space, they decided to rent a small room on the third floor, primarily to store the TV set and seasonal items for the altar. They also agreed to purchase a set of fabric hangings by Adelaide Winsted, a well-known fiber artist outside of Seekers, which would be portable and yet make the worship space more appropriate for us. That signified a growing spirit of identification with art for Seekers. For years, those panels were hung for our worship service and taken down again before the second service.

C OF S FAMILY EXPANDS (1982)

In November of 1982, the New Community Church, pastored by Jim Dickerson, became the seventh C of S church approved by the council. Through FLOC, both Sonya and Fred had worked with Jim, and Seekers felt a close affinity for New Community because it was to be a neighborhood church *with no single mission*. Like Fred in his position at FLOC, Jim was also the director of Manna, the non-profit housing rehab organization where Seekers had been investing their share of C of S bequest money.

With the founding of New Community Church, many Seekers felt they now had a kindred spirit among the C of S communities, and Seekers pledged several thousand dollars to underwrite the budget of New Community during its first year. Some core members raised an uncomfortable question: Were we paying Jim and Grace Dickerson to serve the poor in a drug-infested neighborhood because we weren't able or willing to do it ourselves? Others were just glad to support their neighborhood outreach in the Shaw District, a poor neighborhood beyond the Columbia Road corridor where most of the other C of S ministries were located.

INTENTIONALITY

Giving at Seekers continued to grow as new members joined in the eighties. While there was general agreement on the importance of giving as an act of freedom from the culture, men and women voiced different concerns. For couples where one person was not part of Seekers, the core group finally suggested 5 percent of the household income or 10 percent of the member's individual income. That guideline seemed unjust for men who supported a whole family or earned significantly more than their wives, and we agreed that couples needed to negotiate an appropriate amount for their giving to Seekers, but that tithing one's current income would be the guideline. In the end, the highest value was named as "intentionality and a desire to grow toward releasing individual control of where our money went" by giving to Seekers and then advocating for recipient organizations where we were personally engaged.

When two core members divorced in 1986, the husband confessed that he was in a financial bind and could not give as freely as before. He and his spiritual director agreed that for one year he would give a single silver dollar each week as a reminder of his intentional process. Every Sunday, the sound of that coin dropping into the ceramic offering plate reminded many of us that giving was a spiritual practice designed to support our commitments, not an inflexible law.

In a dilemma unusual for any church, giving toward the end of 1986 was running at a considerably higher rate than the budget. Still committed to zero-base budgeting, our treasurer suggested that Seekers send an extra $10,000 to Dayspring Church and allocate $5,000 to $6,000 for redoing the basement area at 2025. In another unusual gesture, core members authorized a personal loan of $2,740 to a couple in the church. They set up an accountability person and expected regular though small repayment amounts with no interest. Neither person was a core member, but they had been regular participants in the community for several years.

More recently, such loans have become more common as we have drawn more low-income people into the congregation. In each case, an accountability partner was identified to work with the loan recipient on some of the same questions that core members discussed as they worked together on sections of the budget. It was a practice that was designed to encourage transparency and trust.

6

Beliefs That Bind Us Together
Reworking the Commitment Statement

YEARLY RECOMMITMENT WAS A Church of the Saviour practice from the start. It was understood to be our human response to God's call. Core members would stand during worship and read the commitment statement, which was both a profession of faith and a promise to participate wholeheartedly in the community.[1]

When Seekers formed in 1976, that commitment statement was the foundation for trust among the members, since they all belonged to different mission groups outside of Seekers. By 1982, a third of the original members had left and most newcomers belonged to mission groups within Seekers, so the time was ripe for rethinking the response that core members would make to the call of Seekers.

FEMINIST CRITIQUE

Even before Seekers formed, some of the women were interested in updating the language and addressing the hierarchical imagery in the C of S members' statement. In particular, the image of God as "the owner" sitting up on a "throne" did not sit well with Sonya and Emily. They wanted language for a two-way relationship that would speak of freedom and grateful response. They also rejected terms like "sacrificial service" in favor of God as a "lavish giver."

Even though the C of S commitment statement remained in place for several years, Sonya emphasized God's love and generosity in her prayers

---

1. Appendix 1.

during worship. The women's theology group examined the basic theological premises of the core member's commitment from a woman's perspective, and they tried to find new wording to reflect their concerns about inclusion and recognition of ministry in daily life in order to remove the perceived sexism in the C of S membership statement.

A first draft of the rewritten membership statement was circulated among members in August 1982. It raised many issues of inclusive language, belief, and theological understanding. Bob Bayer, who had considered priesthood for himself, submitted an alternative "think piece" on Seekers theology. It started with traditional doctrinal questions like "Who is Jesus? How do we understand the Risen Christ? And what is the Trinity?" Sonya, Liz, and Emily spoke for a more feeling-oriented approach based on the impact of those statements within the community. Others weighed in as well, as it became clear that many of the core members wanted to be involved in the process of developing a coherent theology for Seekers, so the task of rewording the commitment statement would not be an easy one.

When a new membership commitment statement was finally adopted in October 1983, the intention to join Seekers as a core member was linked both to "the tradition of Church of the Saviour" and the worldwide "people of God throughout the ages." The form was creedal, but the content was fresh and inclusive. Regarding Jesus, the traditional death and resurrection language was followed by: "[he] rose from the dead and now bids us to a ministry of love and justice." And the Holy Spirit was acknowledged as "the empowering presence and breath of God [who] confronts and inspires us to do God's work in the world." They also added another important statement of belief about Seekers: "We believe that we are all ministers of the Church, which is both universal, grace-filled body of Christ, and fragile earthen vessel."[2]

When the core members finally approved this new statement of our response to God's call, there was a sense that they had clarified the basic theology of Seekers, at least for the time being.

IS MEMBERSHIP AN ORDINATION?

The question of whether core membership was an ordination process had been alive in Seekers since Fred and Sonya agreed to co-pastor the community. Fred was ordained in a Southern Baptist church, but Sonya and

2. Appendix 5.

other core members served at the Communion table on the basis of their ordination as committed members of Seekers. Gordon Cosby had been clear about wanting to eliminate the line between clergy and laity, but in practice he always presided at the monthly Communion. Once the membership commitment was clarified, another group worked on a "theology of ordination" paper for Seekers. When their report was ready, the study group came out strongly *against* the clericalism implied by denominational ordination. Seekers continued to work on language to acknowledge the sacramental role of core members, without setting them apart too firmly.

In response to the ordination paper, David Lloyd opposed the use of stoles during worship because it set worship leaders apart from the congregation. In his letter, David appealed to the image of Jesus' servanthood and encouraged core members to focus on serving rather than leading. He agreed with those who saw shared leadership as more than the partnership between Fred and Sonya, and his letter was another piece in the growing body of understanding about the *priesthood of all believers*. At that point, the beautiful stole designed by Adelaide Winstead to match the *Tree of Life* hanging was tucked away and used only rarely. Worship leaders had never worn robes at Seekers, and now they would not wear stoles either.

Core members also affirmed the process for receiving new members with the plant ritual designed by Emily Benson, and the language about this being an ordination was eliminated. In response to the changes in the commitment statement, the new receiving statement would say, "We are all ministers," which would be followed by laying on hands as "empowerment for ministry." Within Seekers, we wanted a flat structure of shared leadership, but we wanted to empower our members to function liturgically in other churches too.

CHILDREN AS MISSION

After New Community joined the Church of the Saviour family, Elizabeth O'Connor directed publication of a new booklet that would describe all seven of the churches. Mission groups listed in the booklet for Seekers included five FLOC groups, along with the four internal mission groups described earlier. Fred's full-time work as the director of FLOC continued to inform his preaching, and Sonya's participation in Hope and a Home made it a place where Seekers could nurture other suburbanites toward inner-city ministry. However, because FLOC groups were exempt from the rule that each mission group would have at least two core members, FLOC groups were mostly absent from the attention of other core members. Even the Hope and a Home mission group, where several members of Seekers (including Sonya) were members, did not make a yearly report to the core group. As FLOC became more professional, participation by Seekers gradually diminished as a new cluster of mission groups formed within Seekers.

As the focus on children shifted from FLOC to Seekers, we struggled to find ways for our children to experience an inward and outward spiritual journey themselves. Given the large number of children at Seekers (about forty) and the small size of the adult congregation (about fifty), staffing the Sunday school was always a challenge. After much discussion, a new strategy was adopted. There would be four classes, each taught by a team of four or five adults who would plan and develop the curriculum as well as teach and administer the classes. The teams would function as a support group for their members, and would stay together for half the year. The concept recalled staff teams at The Potter's House, and there was great hope that people would be willing to miss worship if they could develop relationships with the other team members. But, as temporary mission groups on top of other commitments, the effort was too great to sustain, so we went back to recruiting teachers again.

In their effort to make the rituals of worship more accessible to children, Celebration Circle planned a simultaneous Maundy Thursday service in four different homes: one in Maryland, two in the District, and one in Virginia. Using the same liturgy, everyone would gather for foot washing and Communion, which was to be offered by one of the core members in each home. Participation in those separate liturgies was slim, and after that we held a single foot washing service at 2025 on Maundy Thursday. Although we did not succeed in involving most of the children, the effort gave rise to a yearly foot washing service, which is the most intimate and powerful service of the year for some. For others, it is much too intimate. Over time, this Maundy Thursday ritual, followed by a simple meal of dates, figs, and hummus, has become a powerful reminder of Jesus' servant leadership, which we want to cultivate in the whole community.

SHARE THE PULPIT!

Accountability for pastoring and shared preaching in Seekers arose again in the context of recommitment and budget preparation. When Fred and

Anne Taylor quietly divorced in 1985, a pastor's review committee met with Fred and Sonya to look at issues around their roles and responsibilities at Seekers. Committee members worried that Fred's schedule of working full-time at FLOC and two days a week for Seekers left him no time for rest and renewal. They affirmed his interest in outdoor education, and cut his work time for Seekers to one and a half days per week, while Sonya was confirmed at three days a week. Then the review committee offered a strongly worded proposal for Fred to *share the pulpit* regularly with others in the community. In many ways, this signaled the end of the pastoral decade at Seekers.

Since Fred was being paid primarily for his preaching, it was suggested that others should be paid as well. Money was allocated for those honoraria, and core members named half a dozen people whom they thought were qualified to preach in the community. The women's theology group was particularly vocal about wanting more visibility for women in the pulpit, so Fred agreed to ask various women to share his preaching role.

As part of this feminist ferment, Emily Benson officially decided to claim her maiden name, Gilbertson, without the "son" at the end of it. She described it as a response to studying the Gospel of Mark and finding no mention of Mary in the first half. "Women need to claim their own names," she said, and she proceeded to do so legally, even though she and Carl Benson continued their long marriage. We celebrated her name change at the first women's retreat, which was led by Mary Clare Powell at the Wellspring Center. Addressing her as Emily Gilbert from then on was easier because Carl was not involved at Seekers except on ceremonial occasions.

The Festival Center

As Seekers developed a separate identity from Church of the Saviour, Gordon was also developing his vision for other new ministries. Plans for the Festival Center, as a locus for ministries along Columbia Road and home for a new Servant Leadership School, were announced at the C of S council meeting early in 1986. To be completed by 1988, the Festival Center was to be built near The Potter's House on land donated by Jim Rouse, the developer of Columbia, Maryland, and other urban renewal projects in Baltimore and Boston.

The Festival Center seemed to be a whole new initiative now that Gordon was not burdened with managing the multiplicity of groups contained in the original church. In the prospectus, Church of the Saviour was presented as a separate entity without any reference to the sister churches. The Festival Center would be financially and administratively separate, with its own board and staff, unrelated to any of the existing churches or to the C of S council. Ministries to be clustered there were listed in the prospectus.

Festival Center Ministries

1. Cana Industries, providing work opportunities for those needing job skills;
2. Christ House, an infirmary for homeless street people;
3. Columbia Road Health Services, providing medical care for low-income people;
4. Good Shepherd, a program for children of low income families;
5. Jubilee Housing, 358 apartments for low-income people;
6. Jubilee Jobs, job placement for challenged job seekers;
7. Samaritan Inns, transitional housing for otherwise homeless people;
8. Sarah's Circle, affordable housing for low-income elderly.

To Seekers, the Festival Center meant that our hopes for a more vibrant association among the sister churches would be even less likely. We imagined that the Festival Center would house offices of those related ministries, and the second-generation churches would fend for themselves. We also wondered what would become of 2025, where Seekers continued to hold worship and our School of Christian Living.

Some of the other C of S churches were also struggling to find structures that would be able to hold their call in the world. The Columbia Road churches (Eighth Day, Jubilee, and Potter's House) continued to worship at The Potter's House, waiting for the Festival Center to be built. Seekers sent monthly work parties to help Jim Dickerson with renovation of the brick residence on S Street, which would become the home of Manna and the New Community Church. In the fall of 1986, Dunamis Vocations Church decided to end its life as a worshiping community, which brought the number of C of S churches back down to six.

Shortly after that, Dayspring Church reported that the county fire inspection had closed the farmhouse for worship or Bible study, and the Farm Mission Group at Dayspring announced that it was bankrupt, with a

$40,000 debt. In light of the financial crisis at Dayspring, the C of S council faced the question of whether the headquarters building at 2025 could be used as collateral for a loan. Gordon said that, from his perspective, the call of the New Lands process meant that each sister community should be financially self-sufficient. That seemed to settle the matter without addressing the fact that the Dayspring property was owned jointly by all the core members of the different churches. Dayspring Church was left to grapple with its debt.

FORTY YEARS

On October 25, 1987, more than two hundred people gathered at Dayspring to celebrate the fortieth anniversary of Church of the Saviour. Gordon had turned seventy that year, and many people gathered to celebrate his remarkable leadership, as well as a decade of life for the second-generation churches. The day was bright and clear, the fields of Dayspring were freshly mown, and sun sparkled on the Lake of the Saints. Everyone gathered for worship under a large green-and-white striped tent. Seekers took the lead in designing an inclusive liturgy for the occasion, and Sonya held the space as liturgist. All of the associated churches were represented in some way as we celebrated a decade of separate formation in the New Lands. Looking back, we could embrace our common heritage. Looking ahead, we could see growing diversity.

The fortieth anniversary was also marked by a new book by Elizabeth O'Connor. In a change from her earlier books, *Cry Pain, Cry Hope* was less about Church of the Saviour than about her own journey toward claiming a new call. Subtitled *Thresholds to Purpose*, it was a description of how denying her call had been a part of her ten-year struggle with a mysterious crippling illness. Elizabeth's book was confessional and personal about her search for a diagnosis, and her reluctance to embrace a call to housing for low-income seniors, which might require fund-raising for the rest of her life. The book described both her reluctance and her new commitment to provide community and services at Sarah's Circle, a residence for elderly poor people near The Potter's House. By her own admission, Elizabeth's health improved as she embarked on this new call, and she was soon able to drive, to counsel, and to teach again. To those in the wider circle of C of S churches, the book described both the pain and the hope that many people were experiencing in the New Lands process.

7

Open Pulpit
The Spirit Speaks in Many Tongues

QUESTIONS ABOUT SHARED LEADERSHIP took a sharper edge as the community continued to grow. By 1987, regular attendance at worship hovered around sixty adults, but the core group stayed relatively small, at eighteen. There were thirty-six people in small groups, where accountability, confession, and call could be engaged, but that meant nearly half of the adults were in no group, mission or otherwise. There were also forty children on the Sunday school roster, without a coordinator for the children's program. Growth in numbers threatened to overwhelm our capacity for caring.

By then, the pattern had evolved for mission groups to take care of pastoring members of their own group, and for Sonya to pay close attention to those not in mission groups. Knowing that Fred wanted to reduce his time to one day a week and that Sonya was willing to continue at three days a week, a group of core members agreed to undertake a wider inquiry about the aspects of leadership that required paid staff to accomplish. With so many people not in mission groups, there was a general feeling of needing more help for "managing" Seekers organizationally.

SOMEONE FOR CHILDREN?

While the Pastor's Liaison Committee worked with the question of what Seekers needed from paid and unpaid leadership, a new member at Seekers sent a strong letter of support for someone in the community to be hired specifically to encourage ministry to and with children and their families.

"It is not that our current paid ministers are unconcerned about children," she wrote, but "we need someone to build a full pastoral relationship with the children and integrate them more fully into the whole koinonia of Seekers." She wanted a mission group for older children, more activities among families, retreats for children, family enrichment activities, building connection of Seekers children with other C of S children, and some joint programming with FLOC or other inner-city children. She thought the job would be nearly full-time.

The letter raised the issue of paying for leadership in a community where the volunteer resources were many, but often overbooked. Because the call of Seekers specifically included family as a locus of God's call, core members felt obliged to nourish the children in our midst, but we were unwilling to take the conventional path and hire someone from outside of Seekers to do it for us. Neither Sonya nor Fred was called to focus specifically on youth, although Sonya was attentive to support for young families. She spoke often of her belief that there would be someone with those gifts in the community. It was her way of evoking gifts for ministry that might be dormant in someone's heart.

A subtle shift had also taken place in worship. Although Fred continued to determine who would preach and when, women from Seekers were preaching at least half the time. And because Celebration Circle was committed to gender balance at the altar, that shift in preaching meant that Sonya was now sharing her position as liturgist with Peter Bankson, who was writing prayers and leading worship whenever a woman preached. Peter's prayer language was different from Sonya's, but he shared her sense of holding space for the Spirit to work during our extended prayer times in worship. Both used the role of liturgist to introduce many names for God so we wouldn't fall into narrow definitions. In our extended prayer times, both of them offered a bidding prayer for confession, then thanksgiving, and then intercession, each followed by space for spoken prayers from the congregation. Although there was no official recognition of the new pattern, their continuity provided a visible sign of stability as the number of different preachers began to increase.

Although Sonya and Peter were the official liturgists, they drew from the rich process of creating lectionary-based liturgies with others in Celebration Circle. The process invited all members of the group to grow in their awareness of vocal rhythms, poetic language, and consciousness of time and space in worship. When our website was developed, those seasonal liturgies were posted along with weekly sermons, and we discovered that small churches around the world were eager to use them.

When the Pastor's Liaison Committee report was finally presented to the core members, it identified four general areas in which leadership was essential for Seekers: *community growth; commitment to God; building inclusion and trust;* and *deepening our commitment to justice, peace, feminism, and growth*. It ignored the plea for someone to focus on youth. They listed the desired actions to accomplish those goals, but did *not* assume that paid staff was necessary to accomplish all of it.

Another issue was how a larger leadership team might be represented in worship, or not. Since the call of Seekers Church was to be a worshipping community, was worship leadership necessary to develop credibility for new members of the team? Or were the functions separate? Theological reflection was clearly an expectation that we had of Fred and Sonya, but would we want the same from someone who might focus on youth or pastoral care? If so, where would that take place? How would it happen?

TEAM MINISTRY

On September 9, 1988, many Seekers gathered to celebrate Fred's marriage to a member of St. Mark's Episcopal Church on Capitol Hill. Their wedding was a gala occasion with dancing, toasts, and heartfelt wishes for Fred's happiness, but people wondered about his future role at Seekers. He was still working full-time as the director of FLOC, and he was being pressured by the Liaison Committee to give more attention to pastoring newcomers at Seekers.

Following Fred's marriage, Sonya announced to the core members that she believed the word "co-pastor" was no longer the appropriate term for her relationship with Fred, and in order to make room for an additional person on their leadership team she suggested "team ministry" as the appropriate term as we shifted toward a more organizational structure. Perhaps nobody should have been surprised when, at the October members meeting, Fred announced his intention to resign as a paid staff person. He said that he felt his pastoring had become an "annual issue," and that he felt called to "turn loose of the clergy role." He stated his intention to remain an active part of Seekers, but not as one of two pastors. "I want to be off the covert and overt agenda," he said.

Fred's resignation altered the climate for discussion of paid leadership in Seekers. Suddenly our assumptions about needing additional help for youth seemed questionable because we needed to address the primary structure of leadership at Seekers. A new group was formed to assess the leadership needs now that Fred was no longer holding the male/clergy "spot" on the ministry team. His resignation also raised some of the old issues about ordination because we had unconsciously relied on Fred's clergy status, even though it had been conferred by another judicatory.

OPEN PULPIT

In the wake of Fred's resignation, core members decided to open the pulpit to any member of the community rather than trying to replace Fred as our primary preacher. Exercising their authority for worship, Celebration Circle then issued guidelines for preaching. To hold the pulpit space open and still give some structure to our expectations, these guidelines were meant to encourage careful preparation and delivery of sermons:

1. Consider a variety of forms (teaching, prophecy, visioning, participative, nonverbal);
2. Make an explicit connection to the lectionary scriptures for the week;
3. Ground your offering in your theological work;
4. Consider how your offering can build the life of Seekers;
5. Consider how you can invite us to an encounter with God and a relationship with Christ;
6. Consider how you can invite us into a deeper connection with Seekers Church;
7. Consider how you can invite us to an outer journey in mission;
8. Link us to our Christian tradition;
9. Shed light on the meaning of Christian discipleship;
10. Make sure your sermon can be related to the theme for the worship season.

Stalking the Spirit

With the shift to an open pulpit, stipends for preaching were dropped from the budget. Instead, Seekers planned for additional ministry team help. Beyond the allocation for space, members allowed $40,000 for internal needs (mostly staff salaries) and nearly $54,000 for external giving—much more for external giving than the 50-50 rule mandated. FLOC was by far the largest recipient of our domestic giving, with the New Community Church as the next largest. At that time, the health clinic in South Africa was the primary international recipient.

As tensions rose over leadership needs in the wake of Fred's resignation, core members invited everyone to a congregational meeting. About forty people attended, roughly two-thirds of the adult congregation. Nobody wanted to look for a single person to replace Fred as a co-pastor with Sonya, but the connection between prophetic leadership and preaching was in flux. There was some fear that we would settle into a comfortable sense of belonging to a community of faith without the challenge of advocacy for children in the city which Fred had brought to us from FLOC. Could we live up to Robert Greenleaf's challenge as Seekers, and listen deeply enough to hear the prophetic voices in our midst?

A deeper issue that surfaced at the open forum was the link between belonging and decision-making. Mission group members who were not core members pushed for more influence on the question of having paid staff at all. Ron Arms, whose family arrived at Seekers two years before this, was particularly vocal about wanting *no paid staff* and opening the decision-making process to everyone. In response, Sonya described different ways of influencing decisions through mission groups and other task groups. Others felt that the time had come to offer membership to anyone who wanted to choose an intentional spiritual life with an accountability partner. However, to open membership to everyone in Seekers would require changing the membership commitment which we had inherited from Church of the Saviour and had changed only once, in 1983. Nobody was eager to tackle that question along with considering the role of paid leadership in Seekers, so changing our commitment statement was put on the back burner in favor of defining a new ministry team to serve the community along with Sonya.

Open Pulpit

LEADERSHIP OF THE WHOLE

The group studying our leadership needs issued an important policy paper, "Call to Leadership of the Whole." Whoever would join Sonya on a new ministry team would be a generalist, and not a specialist hired for a special function. That was a critical element, because it meant that we would *not* seek a youth specialist. Instead, the committee suggested that we might be looking for an "inclusion pastor" who would work two days a week assisting Sonya with incorporating people who were not in a mission group.

The paper also described the responsibility of core members in a new way: "Each member shares responsibility for the life and health of the Seekers Church . . . through our spiritual gifts." Although Fred and Sonya had worked hard to make the core members responsible for the life and health of Seekers Church, not all of the members took that responsibility seriously. The C of S council had never been responsible for the life and health of the church. Now core members at Seekers were specifically charged with care for the whole community.

The leadership group also made another important statement of policy: "We expect our staff to be committed members of Seekers." In other words, we would not seek paid leadership outside of the circle of core members. The group also recommended one to three paid staff providing up to seven staff days a week—more than we had expected from Fred and Sonya together. In addition, they recommended unpaid staff with a specific call, willing to give a minimum commitment of six hours a week beyond the regular member's commitment of time. By implication, that meant an unpaid staff member for youth. Although they did not address the issue of pay directly, it was clear that they assumed the ministry team would be employed elsewhere and could afford to do this work without dependence on it for a living wage.

After a lively discussion, core members approved the proposal and two men, Peter Bankson and Bob Bayer, dropped off of the leadership committee as they became applicants for the ministry team with Sonya. Then the report and its criteria began to circulate more widely in Seekers.

CHANGE THE CALL OF SEEKERS?

In the middle of this swirl over Fred's resignation and defining our leadership needs, Pat Conover offered a resolution to change the call of Seekers in order to make it more specifically open to "lesbian, gay, bisexual, transvestite, and transexually oriented people." Although some members may have been aware of Pat's transgender identity at that time, it was not obvious from his dress, nor had he discussed it with the core members. When he suggested this change to the call, minutes of that meeting record an awkward and confused discussion about whether the call needed to be changed, and if so, how. Inclusion had always been a high value at Seekers, but the focus had been toward gender equity and the inclusion of children, rather than on racial or sexual reconciliation. The relevant language of the call stated inclusiveness this way: "The Seekers community sees itself called into Christ's ministry of deliverance from bondage to freedom in every personal and corporate expression."[1]

At that point, the call of Seekers Church had never been changed, although the commitment statement had been revised in 1983 to make it more inclusive. As usual when such a large question arose, a special group was formed to study the call of Seekers and make specific recommendations about whether to change the wording as Pat suggested. At that time, Pat was working full-time on issues of public advocacy for the UCC denomination, but he had not yet published his book, *Transgender Good News*. The issue of changing the language of our call became tangled with the discussion of decision-making authority until the new ministry team finally sorted it out.

NEW MINISTRY TEAM

In April 1989, a new staff team was selected and confirmed by the core members. The open pulpit was confirmed as well. Peter Bankson and Kay Schultz were to be paid for working one day a week, Bob Bayer was confirmed for two days a week, and Sonya would continue at three days a week at her higher salary rate. Kay had been working with Jim Dickerson at Manna for many years and the Schultzes had two teenage daughters at Seekers. She began working immediately with the "New Age Group" of teens and saw her primary focus as inclusion of younger people, even though all staff members were called to "care for the whole" instead of dividing up their time into functional areas. Peter and Bob were both retired military officers, devoted Seekers, and capable generalists with strong management skills. Both had jobs that would allow them time for the ministry team. Bob

---

1. Appendix 3.

was then working for the Senate Armed Services Committee, and Peter was at Communities in Schools, a national dropout prevention program.

There was no attempt to describe the new team members as pastors, even though pastoring had been the need expressed for more of Fred's time. Instead, core members affirmed Sonya's pastoring skills, and named mission groups as the other source of care and accountability in Seekers. By implication, then, Sonya would continue to pastor those not in mission groups, the men would bring their organizational skills, and Kay would guide the youth program. All through this process, Fred continued to participate as a core member of Seekers—watching and listening as we moved to a new form of team leadership around Sonya.

8

Team Leadership
Encouraging Commitment for All

THE QUESTION OF HOW much structure was needed to hold together this *do-it-ourselves* church was central as the new leadership team moved into place in 1989. With about seventy adults and nearly forty children in the congregation, circle time before worship was loud and boisterous. Newcomers clamored to have a say in community decisions, and the new staff team worked hard to guide the whole community toward deepening our culture of commitment.

Seekers' call named the importance of gathering for worship and dispersing for ministry in daily life. Most Seekers did, in fact, find a sense of call in their paid work outside of the community. Others experienced God's call in family, volunteer work, or other creative activities. Those in mission groups had a weekly opportunity to bring the spiritual aspect of their work and family life into consciousness through their written reports and verbal sharing, but others did not. How to weave our many calls into the whole fabric of Seekers remained ambiguous, although the newly opened pulpit offered some opportunities for that.

CHANGING THE CALL

After Pat Conover proposed a change to the call of Seekers in order to specifically welcome LGBT persons, core members focused several meetings on sexuality as a spiritual issue. There had never been any opposition to welcoming gays and lesbians at Seekers, and the original call had affirmed "differing lifestyles" as a justice issue, so changing the call seemed unnecessary to some. The spirit of Seekers on this issue was to accept people as God made them and expect everyone to be respectful of each other.

By September 1989, Peter reported that the staff team was ready to recommend a change in our call in order to make Seekers a more welcoming community. Assuming that they had the power to change the call without consulting the congregation, the core members approved a two-sentence addition:

> We desire and welcome participation in Seekers Church of women and men of every race and sexual orientation. We recognize the value of each individual and seek to heal any wounds of discrimination inflicted by our society and church.

Core members did not foresee the firestorm that changing our call would cause among others in the congregation who were not consulted. In a strongly worded letter to the core group, David Lloyd challenged the changes they had approved. He wanted the call of Seekers to represent a "consensus of the Seekers faith community" and not just the core members. He found the process "secretive" and wanted a more open and inclusive process in the future. As a lawyer engaged with helping victims of exploitive sexual behavior, he was particularly concerned about the second sentence of the change. He said that, in his experience, pedophiles frequently pointed to their sexual orientation as a rationalization for their behavior, and he urged some identification of the types of sexual behavior that Seekers would not welcome.

To find some ground for reconciliation, all Seekers were encouraged to come on the spring overnight at Wellspring, where we would have time and space to discuss the changes that had been made to the call. Once there, adults earnestly tried to bridge the gap between core members and regular attenders around how changes to the call were to be made, while the children raced around the grounds of Dayspring Farm. It was a conscious attempt to listen deeply but not give away the power to make those changes.

Wording of the change to Seekers' call continued to irritate some of the regular attenders, but Pat held firmly to his desire for the wording that had been adopted, even though it was more general than what he had originally proposed. Because the School of Christian Living on Tuesday nights was one place where everyone could engage with specific topics, it became a locus for broader discussion of these community issues. After much debate and discussion about our functional welcome for gay, lesbian, bisexual, and transgender people, core members decided to move the second sentence, "We recognize the value of each individual and seek to heal any wounds of discrimination inflicted by our society and church," to a different paragraph of the Seekers call. Words referring to unlawful behavior were not included.[1]

MONEY AS A MATTER OF FAITH

In the midst of this furor over changing the call of Seekers, other people were anxious to continue cultivating a spirit of collective generosity with our money. Some people were concerned that increasing the size of our staff team meant that we would lose our passion for outreach giving, even though it had grown from 40 percent of the total in 1977 to 50 percent of a larger total in 1989. Ron Arms asked for $500 from the Growing Edge Fund to put in the collection plate for people to take in order to experiment with receiving as well as giving. As a former pastor himself, Ron wanted Seekers to be an all-volunteer community with no paid leadership, but the core members were unwilling to revisit their long practice of paying the ministry team a modest stipend. They questioned whether volunteers could sustain the effort to build a discipling community with strong financial support.

Interest in giving to places where Seekers members were directly involved continued to grow as new people joined the congregation. Several brought international connections through the World Bank and other governmental agencies. As we began to look for a place where Seekers might develop a mission trip that would include young people, the core members approved these guidelines for assessing program submissions and recommending outreach allocations in the budget:

> Guidelines for International Giving
>
> 1. support sustainable development;
>
> 2. benefit women and children;
>
> 3. be a place of direct Seeker involvement;
>
> 4. go to an organization rather than an individual (Christian if possible).

---

1. Appendix 4.

The guidelines placed a high value on giving to structures for social change rather than to direct aid or charity. Unlike the other C of S churches, Seekers did not funnel money into a single project like housing or healthcare. Focus on benefits for women and children reflected the feminist concerns of Seekers. The parenthetical reminder that we would seek organizations that were "Christian if possible" recognized the value of servant organizations while acknowledging that God's work in the world might take other, more secular, forms as well. The interest in "sustainable development" affirmed our preference for policy and structures.

STRENGTHENING THE CORE GROUP

As 1989 came to a close, the core members went on retreat together at Wellspring—the first retreat since Seekers formed in 1976. At the retreat, Kate Cudlipp read her spiritual autobiography, which brought the core membership total up to twenty-one. Only six had been founding members; the rest had been shaped and schooled by Seekers.

The new ministry team gained visibility at the retreat, and it marked the beginning of a more organizational period for Seekers. A clear confirmation process for youth was presented by Kay. There would be four weekend retreats to help the teens understand their heritage in the Christian tradition along with the inward/outward journey of Church of the Saviour. The youth would formulate their own belief statements, as well as experience a mission project. The pattern of weekend retreats, rather than Sunday morning classes, proved to be very effective for building a cohesive group of young teens at Seekers. Now grown, many of those young adults return for Christmas and Easter reunions at Seekers.

Bob and Peter brought their administrative skills by creating an "agenda bush" to make the issues being considered by the core group more visible to the community. Since there was no newsletter or website at the time, the agenda bush was posted on an upstairs bulletin board, along with a paper for each item, written by a sponsoring advocate from the group of core members. It was one way of inviting the wider circle of members to interact with those sponsors or add items to the agenda.

After the retreat, Peter staffed publication of the first *Seekers Directory*, and also the *Mission Group Guide*. In order to forestall criticism by the wider community, he circulated sections of the *Guide* as they were developed, and the whole group met often until they were satisfied with the descriptions. The *Mission Group Guide* was an important public statement of mission groups as our primary structures for belonging and spiritual formation, and another way to document our culture of shared leadership and generous giving for newcomers as we moved toward more definable structures.

ORDINATION AND LICENSING

Even though language about membership being an ordination had been removed from the commitment statement, core members wanted Sonya and Peter to legalize their authority to perform marriages now that Fred was no longer on the staff. It was a decision to exercise the provision for ordination that was recommended in the 1983 policy paper. Gordon Cosby signed the letter, authorizing Sonya and Peter to be licensed by the District of Columbia under the auspices of Church of the Saviour. There were also several other people in Seekers who were authorized to perform marriages by virtue of their denominational ordination, but we wanted that legal authority for one or two members of the ministry team.

Relations with Church of the Saviour staff continued to be cordial but not close. The large number of children at Seekers meant that our coffee hour upstairs at 2025 frequently disturbed the initial silence at the second service downstairs, where Gordon was preaching. The issue of financial support for the C of S budget was also a sore spot. When Elizabeth O'Connor contacted Sonya to ask about increasing the contribution that Seekers was making to the C of S budget, Peter prepared a long list of repairs at 2025 that had been made by Seekers and places within the wider C of S community where Seekers were giving money. Apparently their concerns were allayed, because no further question was raised about the Seekers' financial contribution to the overall C of S budget.

Without a single preacher in the pulpit, Sonya and Peter (as liturgists) became the primary spiritual guides for the wider community during this period. When Celebration Circle reported on preaching for the first year with an open pulpit, there had been twenty-two women, twenty-four men, and five groups. Core members preached thirty-four times, twelve sermons were preached by regular attenders, and there were only two outside guest preachers. People took their preaching responsibilities seriously and the community welcomed the variety. Because of the large number of different preachers, the School of Christian Living became the place for more sustained teaching and encouraging deeper commitment.

AUTHORITY AND DECISION-MAKING

In response to the furor over changing Seekers' call, Pat initiated a task force on authority and decision-making. Although he had been ordained by the UCC denomination, Pat was opposed to anything that looked like clerical authority. When the task force made its report, they noted that core members did need some better ways of gathering input from "non-members" for critical issues, but Pat defended the boundary of our strong membership commitment. For Pat, the difference between members and regular attenders was the issue of being "fully committed." For others, the difference was not so clear. There were members who were not fully committed and non-members who were. However, like a marriage ceremony, the commitment statement made a public declaration of accountability which we had come to rely on.[2]

Bob and Peter continued posting a visual "agenda bush" so the whole community could see what the members would be discussing at their monthly meetings. Although the meetings were still closed in an effort to build trust and deepen connections with each other, the staff team (who were also core members) was making a real effort to make the process more visible to everyone.

Inclusion of children was not on the agenda bush, because Kay Schultz saw that as her primary concern. Although the staff team was selected to "care for the whole," Kay was, in fact, more responsible for including the children. She reported that the youth were working at The Potter's House one night a month, helping at a Manna construction site, and beginning a recycling project. And, as a variation on the theme of opening membership to everyone, Celebration Circle began to work on a range of simple rituals that the youth might want to use in order to formalize some kind of membership for the youth at Seekers.

What did not show up on the agenda bush were the resilient connections in our communal life: creative worship, lots of individual call and mission in the workplace, and a quiet dedication to spiritual disciplines of prayer, journaling, and financial generosity. Kay and John Schultz were

2. Appendix 5.

particularly good at inviting Seekers to informal gatherings that were open to all—for dancing, hiking, kayaking, and picnics together.

Core members welcomed Kate Cudlipp's announcement that she would be attending a convocation of gay and lesbian Christians at Kirkridge Retreat Center in June 1991, and they decided to commission her at worship so she would go with the ability to represent Seekers there. Sending Kate to the convocation with our official blessing was the beginning of our "ribbon ceremony." Since then, we have commissioned people with a ribbon as they have made a major life transition, left for a mission trip, or represented Seekers in some other venue, as a sign of our prayers and support. Often, a bit of that ribbon would be left on the prayer net that hangs on the back wall of the sanctuary.

FAMILY MATTERS

That same month, Seekers received a poignant letter from the little church at Dayspring. After nearly forty years, the farmland that Church of the Saviour had purchased near Germantown, Maryland, was no longer in the country. Housing developments pressed in on every side, and because farm operations at Dayspring had ceased, their tax status had been changed. Dayspring Church had signed a one-year farm lease for 1991, but they realized that they might be taxed at the suburban residential rate the following year, which they simply could not afford. Dayspring proposed a process of discernment that would include all C of S members (core members in the sister churches, plus Gateway and Wellspring mission groups). Several core members said they would definitely participate, indicating once again our readiness to support efforts that would involve the related churches in a common cause.

Other C of S churches were also forming along Columbia Road, near The Potter's House. Christ House, the infirmary for street people, gave birth to Christ House Church in 1988. Out of the Festival Center, Festival Church was organized in 1990, and shortly afterward, Lazarus House Church joined the council, bringing the total number of C of S churches to nine. Of those, Dayspring, Seekers, and New Community were geographically separate from the others on Columbia Road, and seemed to be developing more fully as separate churches. Most importantly, all three had their own schools to prepare people for core membership. The Columbia Road churches relied more on Gordon's preaching at the ecumenical service,

Team Leadership

which was still being held at 2025, where Seekers also held worship earlier on Sunday mornings. The Thursday night School of Christian Living had been absorbed by the Servant Leadership School at the Festival Center, but preparing people for membership in the Columbia Road churches was not a high priority. Instead, basic courses in call and community were designed for a broader population to focus on mission and social change.

GUIDE TO SEEKERS CHURCH

The first *Guide to Seekers Church* was published in August 1991. It codified our practices and made our culture of commitment more accessible to everyone. The introduction described our basic values:

> As one of the CoS [sic] faith communities, the life of Seekers Church is based on an amazing belief: Each one of us is called by God to a particular area of service. Young or old; regardless of experience, skills or education; despite our past success or failures—God issues each of us an individual call. Broadly defined, it is a call to a life of love and service.
>
> Coming into membership is an ordination of the new member to a position of leadership within Church of the Saviour. We believe in the priesthood of all believers, and embody that in our belief that committed members are ordained to take sacramental as well as administrative leadership for Seekers.

Nine mission groups were listed in the *Guide*. Of those groups, three were focused mainly on the inner life of Seekers. Six gathered people around a functional specialty for outward mission, and all of them deepened relationships through sharing a common task. Because we depended on mission groups to provide pastoral care for their members, those nine mission groups gave a specific place of belonging for approximately fifty adults, about two-thirds of the congregation at that time. But that still left a large number of people within Seekers without any formal affiliation or designated place of belonging.

With the help of the new staff team, Sonya pushed again to open membership to anyone in Seekers who wanted to be intentional about their spiritual growth. The staff took unilateral action by publishing the invitation in the bulletin during recommitment season in 1991. As a first step toward opening the category of member to everyone, the statement was simple and direct. It claimed Seekers as "my church" and named a desire to be "intentional and accountable" as a "growing Christian."[3]

Comparing the general membership statement to the core members' commitment, two major differences stand out. Core members make a clear statement of belief in "God as triune being," and they commit themselves to carry responsibility for the overall life and health of the whole community. Core members also accept the disciplines of study, prayer, written reports, retreats, and tithing. That it had taken fifteen years to expand the definition of "member" beyond the explicit commitments made by core members indicates how strong the C of S tradition of committed membership was at Seekers. And the fact that the new ministry team decided to make this change without endless discussions suggests a new level of confidence from within the team.

As part of this emerging self-definition, Pat circulated two papers on Seekers as a "community of call." After a period of expansion that brought in a number of new members, he wrote, "we are entering a period when we need to put more emphasis on centering around what holds us together." He named that as being a Christian community defined by *the whole of our callings*. There was no real debate over our identity as a Christian community, although we occasionally had people who wanted to drop "Christian" from the School of Christian Living. Celebration Circle made sure that their creative liturgies were based on the lectionary scriptures, and we expected preachers to follow the lectionary and wrestle with the call to be disciples of Jesus as well as hunters of the Holy Spirit. But how to know the "whole of our callings" was not easy or simple. Although people in mission groups wrote about the "whole of their callings" in weekly written reports, Seekers outside of mission groups had no way of bringing this into the mix of our congregational life except through preaching, Growing Edge partnerships, and informal accountability relationships.

SEXUALITY AND COMMITMENT

From the beginning, Seekers had tried to hold the positive sense of male/female differences, sexual energies, and relational connections, along with good boundaries. Sonya had frequently named the value of acknowledging sexual energies as a source of action and compassion, along with her feminist challenge around gender roles. Her report of working with

3. Appendix 7.

several families on "deep theological issues" suggested her role as a confessor. Members knew that some of the issues she was holding were, in fact, related to sexual behavior and appropriate boundaries.

Given the gender and sexuality issues that had been swirling around Seekers since Pat's proposed change to Seekers' call to specifically welcome gay, lesbian, trans and bisexual people, Ron Arms offered to preach an unprecedented series of six sermons in a row during Pentecost on sexuality. After meeting for nearly a year with the Sexuality & Spirituality mission group, Ron wanted to broaden the discussion of sexuality beyond gender identity and homosexuality, and he wanted to preach a series of sermons on "the body as dialogue with the divine."

In one of those sermons, Ron offered the relationship vision that he and his wife, Julie, had written when they married. Their list spoke to the value of mutual commitment and sexual fidelity in Seekers:

- We discuss our feelings openly. We trust each other's capacity to make choices.

- We are sexually exclusive.

- We share with each other emotional, spiritual and sexual attachments we may develop with others.

- We laugh frequently. We fight fair.

- We encourage each other to grow. We re-evaluate our rules periodically.

- We share important decisions. We affirm and support each other.

- We are loving parents, generous with ourselves and our time.

- We live within our means.

This commitment statement was shared in a class titled "Relationships with Room to Grow," which most of the younger couples in Seekers attended, and everyone in the class affirmed these principles for any committed relationship in Seekers.

As though to incarnate those promises, a wedding provided everyone with a joyous reason to party at Dayspring. Many people from Seekers gathered on a gorgeous day to celebrate the marriage of Margreta Voskuilen and Jeffrey Silverstone. He was dashing in his kilt; she was stunning in a traditional gown. Now that he was officially licensed by the DC government, Peter officiated at the wedding and David Lloyd, the moderator of her mission group, was the master of ceremonies for the folk-dancing party afterward at the outdoor pavilion. Their wedding and dancing party afterward was also a celebration of the new generation of younger people stepping toward shared leadership at Seekers.

GIVING AS A SIGN OF HEALTH

If giving is some indication of health in a church, then Seekers was vitally alive even though there was considerable turmoil within. Because of our commitment not to carry funds from one year to the next, core members had the delightful task of allocating $10,000 in surplus funds. Perhaps it was the glow of that good news that prompted the core group to offer one member $2,500 to write up a report on the Christian education program that she had developed for Seekers. Health benefits were added for Sonya and Kay, and extra amounts were given to the Rolling Ridge Retreat Center and Dayspring Church for maintenance of the retreat facilities.

Periodic bequests to Church of the Saviour continued to be divided among the C of S council members, and when the treasurer announced the receipt of $27,000 from such a bequest division, the entire amount was put in the Manna Capstone Fund. From time to time after 1992, Seekers added more bequest money to the Manna loan and it became a de facto capital fund. We specifically did not use bequests for current operations.

GROWING EDGE

Since 1982, the Growing Edge Fund had quietly offered people a modest amount of money to try something new. A decade later, Billy Amoss asked for a larger amount to launch a project that would provide basic medical supplies for a children's hospital in St. Petersburg, Russia. In his application, he wrote:

> I was in St. Petersburg to supervise the delivery of food aid from the U.S. and heard that this hospital, which was to receive some of the food, was in a state of desperation because the supply line from Moscow . . . has been cut off with the dissolution of the Soviet Union last December. . . . My efforts to organize a project of comprehensive emergency assistance became a personal mission.

> For the first time, my spiritual journey and the work which I do are beginning to be integrated, and for this coming together of what have always been distinct and unrelated areas of my life I feel excitement and deep gratitude.

Sonya and Liz were clearly pleased with Billy's excitement about his new call, and they continued to meet with him as he began to explore the possibilities of working with Mstislav Rostropovich, then the conductor of the National Symphony Orchestra, who wanted to do something for children in St. Petersburg. Within a year, Billy had left his job to direct the new Rostropovich Foundation and the core members who had approved the larger grant felt like they had made a real investment in Billy's response to God's call.

In their capacity as stewards of the Growing Edge Fund, Sonya and Liz also authorized money to help finance a cross-country trip to develop one man's drawing skills, gave money for a first sacred dance workshop, and granted funding to see whether another might explore being a full-time artist. That meant over-subscribing the budget allocation for Growing Edge, but nobody seemed to mind. The road-trip artist courted a woman in Seekers who cared for a severely handicapped child; they eventually married and adopted three children with special needs. The sacred dancer was instrumental in bringing InterPlay to Seekers. The woman who wanted to explore art has become a faculty member at Wesley Theological Seminary and the director of the Dadian Gallery there. In 1992, the Growing Edge Fund was ripe with seeds!

9

New Wineskins
Reshaping Church of the Saviour

GORDON COSBY STUNNED EVERYONE at the C of S council meeting in October 1992 by questioning whether there was enough common ground to hold the C of S faith communities together: "We need new wineskins for new wine," he said. "We now have nine communities. There is growing divergence among them; oneness cannot be maintained."

Gordon recommended that Church of the Saviour be dissolved, and that a new legal structure be developed to permit each faith community to operate with total autonomy, along with a separate corporation to hold any common property. Then each community was invited to incorporate separately and be responsible for any property it had acquired. At a Dayspring gathering, Gordon continued to promote dissolution of C of S with language that seemed to validate the path that Seekers had chosen: "I want us to die our way into a new future. We are called to BE CHURCH. Without stronger Schools of Christian Living, our future will be mediocre. Mission is crucial, but common life is the most important!"

Gordon's call to strengthen the School of Christian Living (SCL) in each community encouraged Seekers, where the SCL often provided a place for discussion of common issues and integration of newcomers. He seemed to be speaking directly to the call of Seekers to *be church*, which had been so suspect in earlier years. In fact, Gordon's speech gave Seekers hope that other related churches might be interested in following the path toward shaping a separate identity, a path which we had been taking for more than fifteen years.

SELL 2025?

With dissolution of Church of the Saviour an impending possibility, Fred Taylor and others sparked an effort to start an emergency medical fund for the three C of S staff members and their spouses (Gordon and Mary Cosby, Bill and Sunny Branner, and Elizabeth O'Connor), who were not covered by Medigap or other supplemental funding. Gordon had staunchly refused such medical insurance, saying that retirement was a secular concept, but Fred felt it was simply right to offer them a backup system in case of emergencies. Representatives from Seekers, New Community, Gateway, and Lazarus House volunteered to administer a Faithful Servants Trust Fund. As the hospitality group for the ecumenical service, Gateway favored funding the trust if 2025 was sold, and the others concurred. This was the first official mention of selling 2025 since the New Lands process began in 1976.

For Seekers, the possibility of C of S dissolution meant that we would lose our place of worship at 2025, because we assumed that the council would put the building up for sale immediately. Impending displacement made our Christmas celebration in 1992 more important than ever. By then, the Christmas Eve potluck supper was a ten-year tradition at Seekers, and it had evolved into an extended gathering of families and young adults who were eager to see one another. That year, food was extravagant, singing fervent, and the candlelight service sent us home in tears.

SECOND EXODUS

After years of quarterly or semi-annual meetings, the Church of the Saviour council began meeting every month to determine the future structure of C of S. Gordon called it "our Second Exodus."

Although Seekers had charted an independent path since 1976, Gordon's push toward separate incorporation seemed like an invitation to sever our ties with the other communities. Since we were not part of the Columbia Road ministries, which clustered around the Festival Center and The Potter's House, we had not been privy to whatever talk about dissolution might have circulated there. It felt like the grand old brownstone, which had held our worship life for so long, was to be left behind in this Second Exodus.

Bill Price, representative of Dayspring to the C of S council, researched the legal documents of incorporation for an interpretation of how dissolution might proceed. According to the constitution, a vote to dissolve the church would require a majority vote of all "members in good standing." In a letter dated March 20, 1993, the nine churches (plus Gateway, a C of S mission group) were listed, along with the number of core members who could vote:

- Christ House (12)
- Dayspring Church (15)
- Eighth Day (18)
- Festival Church (10)
- Jubilee Church (11)
- Lazarus House (4)
- New Community (8)
- Potter's House (23)
- Seekers (21)
- Gateway (3)

Looking at this list, it was obvious that the Columbia Road grouping (Christ House, Eighth Day, Festival, Jubilee, Lazarus House, Potter's House, and Gateway) had more than enough votes to determine what would happen to 2025. Even though individual members could vote separately, Seekers anticipated that the Columbia Road churches would vote for Gordon's proposal to dissolve C of S.

Core members of Seekers responded by holding an open forum for anybody in Seekers to express their concerns or ideas about the future of Seekers within Church of the Saviour. Gordon Cosby attended, but Elizabeth O'Connor declined the invitation to participate, saying she would have "nothing to add." Old issues surfaced. Seekers wanted an inclusive and transparent process that would be open to guidance from the Holy Spirit, while Gordon focused on his call rather than a consultative process.

During the turmoil over what would happen to 2025 if Church of the Saviour disbanded, Bob Bayer asked to drop his staff time back to one day a week, and Kay Schultz took leave from the staff team for the summer as she and her husband tried to sort out family difficulties and his move from government work to full-time carpentry. Suddenly, it looked like Sonya and Peter would be carrying most of the leadership responsibilities for the staff team, although Bob continued to work with them for a while.

When Kay left the staff team in 1993, a position description was circulated by the Liaison Committee for a "leader for children's education." S/he would meet with the leadership team regularly, but not necessarily be on the leadership team. No compensation was included in the description. Although the shift was subtle, the job description for a "children's education leader" referred to the "leadership team" instead of using the carefully chosen title of "staff team."

Most people did refer to Sonya and Peter as "the leadership team." They were, in fact, providing spiritual leadership for the community as the regular liturgists on Sunday, as well as providing administrative leadership for the core group. Even before Bob and Kay resigned, Peter and Sonya were more visible than the other two. Expecting them to provide other kinds of leadership in the community was an easy line to cross without thinking, especially for people who came from more traditional churches and did not sit with them as peers in the circle of core members

When Bob resigned later that year, it prompted another round of discussion about why we paid for a part-time staff team at Seekers. Although some people still wanted a flat structure with a volunteer staff, Sonya defended their stipend, saying payment was "to have some authority when it's needed." Peter suggested that we pay staff members for "their breadth of attention and interruptibility." At that time, both Sonya and Peter had other jobs, so the issue of "interruptibility" was important. Sonya was working two days a week with Jackie McMakin at the Lay Ministry Lab, and Peter was still working full-time at Communities in Schools.

Kate Cudlipp then expressed her sense of call to the leadership team at Seekers. She had been part of the community for ten years, chaired the FLOC board, been part of the Sexuality & Spirituality mission group at Seekers, participated in LGBT retreats at Kirkridge, and completed her Masters in Theological Studies at Wesley Seminary. She also lived in the Adams Morgan district, near The Potter's House, and was serving as the chair of the C of S council. A trained lawyer, Kate had recently retired from staffing the Senate Committee on the Environment, so she offered to work two days a week for Seekers. Core members approved her call unanimously, and Kate joined Sonya and Peter as part of the leadership team in November 1993.

C OF S ASSOCIATION?

The question posed by Gordon about the future form of Church of the Saviour evolved into whether it would be dissolved, become an association of independent churches, or take another form entirely. Congregational ownership of 2025 and Dayspring Farm made complete dissolution difficult to consider, but not impossible.

John Cook, who later became the director of L'Arche in Washington, DC, proposed an association of communities with no paid staff. The C of S council had just refused to add John's Covenant Community to the council because their own future was uncertain, but his suggestion resonated with Seekers. Our representatives, Peter and Kate, embraced the idea of an association. Seekers hoped that 2025 could be retained as a center for common efforts on a newsletter, a bookstore, retreats, an annual celebration at Dayspring, and the C of S healthcare trust fund. We envisioned Seekers as the long-term steward of 2025 in the same way that Dayspring Church had been granted stewardship of the property at Dayspring Farm.

On June 10, 1994, Gordon sent a letter to all core members in the sister communities, giving us two choices: "to let go of Church of the Saviour (or) to reform it into some kind of association." Gordon clearly favored his own proposal to let go of the old structure entirely. In spite of much effort by Seekers, the overwhelming vote was for "gradual release of the Church of the Saviour," rather than for maintaining an umbrella structure.

What that vote meant for Seekers was a loss of place! As the only one of the sister churches still worshipping at 2025, we assumed that if C of S was going to dissolve, the old mansion would soon be sold, and that Gordon would move his office to the Festival Center on Columbia Road. Sonya voiced her disappointment in a strong letter to Gordon, accusing him of choosing fragmentation instead of cooperation.

Gordon responded with his own sense of call and faithfulness, inviting Sonya to share his letter with Seekers. At the age of seventy-seven, Gordon was articulate about his own vision for the church, and he claimed his own limits rather than fragmentation as he wrote back to Sonya:

> It seems to me that our congregational vote does not preclude those who may be called from giving guidance, leadership, confrontation, and support for our various communities that you have expressed sadness over losing. Those who are called to such leadership will give it. Those who long for it will respond.

Gordon's letter seemed to hold the door ajar for Seekers to offer leadership in some new form of Church of the Saviour. However, most of the members who had been sitting in the room when the vote was taken felt that Seekers should make immediate plans to find another home. We began by filing papers for separate incorporation, as did the other communities.

REIMAGINING SEEKERS

Learners & Teachers (L&T) responded to the June vote by designing a single class for all Seekers to attend. L&T agreed that the school could be our forum for community participation and they outlined one class with what they felt were the key issues. Ultimately however, L&T offered four different classes with the express purpose of involving everyone in Seekers. The mission group was confident that suggestions growing out of these classes would be received as strong guidance for our future life together, and nearly everybody in Seekers attended one of those four classes.

The belonging class drew most of the regular attenders, who were interested in finding more official ways of participating. They did affirm the need for core members to carry responsibility for the life of Seekers, glad that anyone could become a member of that group if they felt called to it. The decision-making class grappled with questions of authority and accountability. They pressed for open core member meetings, which we now practice. The stewardship class dealt with gifts of time and energy to overcome the barrier that tithing might present in the context of faith and commitment. The sacred space class looked first at how being at 2025 all these years might have shaped us, and held out visions that other locations would shape us differently. Their recommendation was to make another effort to take on stewardship of 2025.

In the middle of all this angst over reforming Church of the Saviour, Pat Conover and Trish Nemore were married at Wellspring. The beautiful space where we had come for so many community overnights was aglow with candlelight, Christmas greens, and flowers. There were clowns, balloons, hand-woven stoles for the wedding party, and a banquet after the ceremony. Once again, these personal rituals of sacrament and blessings seemed to be a way for the whole body of Seekers to celebrate being together even as external pressures threatened to pull us apart.

DUAL MEMBERSHIP

To prepare for another rare meeting of all Church of the Saviour members on January 22, 1995, Gordon sent a letter to the C of S council stating that the congregational meeting would amend the constitution to allow for dual membership by all certified core members. The letter said, "This arrangement would imply no additional members in the central CoS structures beyond those so certified as of November 20, 1994."

The council was to continue as the decision-making body, and business would be conducted by unanimous vote of the council members present at the meeting, or else be brought to the whole congregation. All three of these proposals—dual membership, decision-making by the council, and operating by consensus—were passed. In practice, the decision about dual membership meant that there would be a steadily decreasing body of decision-makers for C of S as time went on, since no new members could be added.

In response to these changes in the polity of Church of the Saviour, Muriel Lipp wrote a long open letter to all Seekers in February 1995. By then, she was almost seventy and had been a devoted member of C of S before helping to found Seekers. As an elder in this small community, her words had the power to bless our new direction as she described our history to the present moment:

> We followed the thread of women's rights into the poor countries of the world with our money and tried to make our international contributions reflective of our belief that women's cooperatives in Africa and Latin America were the way to help oppressed nations.
>
> We also followed our interest in families into the arena of sexuality. What is sexuality in God's plan? From there we went to sexual orientation, seeing gay people as oppressed, inviting them through our bulletin to join us. All of this was done through our worship, our SCL classes and a new group, Sexuality and the Spirit.
>
> I would like to see us continue to explore vocational ministry as corporate mission. Our Public Policy Group is doing this. Mission Support Group is also doing it. For our many career families in Seekers, this enables them to be on mission in the world and still help out with the family income. It is not the CoS model, which is to set up a mission that the called can staff. In this we are revisionist. But then, the gifts God has given us are different too—40 children, most of whom will go to college. The costs are staggering to parents, and that impinges on us.

Muriel affirmed our different needs and a different understanding of the Spirit's leading. Where that would take place was still an open question because the future of 2025 had not yet been decided.

With optimism over the possibility of an association, Seekers began to imagine long-term stewardship of the headquarters building at 2025 as a center for liturgy and the arts, a resource center for small church liturgy, inclusive children's curricula and mission, a center for ministry in daily life, a center for lay leadership and small group leadership training, a prayer vigil ministry at the midpoint between the Capitol and the National Cathedral, a resource center for spirituality in international development, an incubation center for new ministries, and focused outreach to the surrounding gay and lesbian community. Although none of those uses were aimed at the poor and marginalized of the city, Seekers knew that 2025 had never been the primary place of mission for Church of the Saviour either.

On February 19, 1995, Seekers sent a letter to the C of S council formally asking to become the long-term steward of the headquarters building at 2025 Massachusetts Avenue. Meanwhile, the council began to deed titles to properties owned by C of S to various ministries that had, in fact, raised the funds for these missions. The property at 614 S Street went to New Community Church, and 2474 Ontario went to the L'Arche community. The Potter's House building was deeded to Potter's House Church.

At that point, there seemed to be a fairly equal split between selling 2025 and keeping it. To some, offering short-term stewardship to Seekers seemed to be a suitable compromise between selling it immediately and keeping it until Gordon was ready to stop preaching at the ecumenical service. Within Seekers however, there was considerable opposition to accepting short-term stewardship if we would just have to move in three more years.

New Community and Dayspring affirmed Seekers' call to general stewardship of 2025. Eighth Day, Jubilee, and Festival Church affirmed a three-year stewardship plan for Seekers. Gateway wanted to sell 2025 immediately and fund the Faithful Servants Trust. Christ House and Lazarus House were also more concerned about the ecumenical staff, and they also supported selling the building to fund the Servants Trust first, then to divide the remaining proceeds for mission.

STEWARDS OF DAYSPRING

On April 23, 1995, the C of S council received a formal request from Dayspring Church to take on stewardship of the whole farm property (except for the Wellspring conference center and associated cabins). The letter included dreams for deepening their community life, widening outreach, maintaining silent retreat, providing a visible earth-keeping witness, and reaching out to "the marginalized as well as our D.C. and international neighbors." Dayspring named six mission groups, plus Ministry of Money and World Peacemakers, as part of their outreach. Quietly and without fanfare, a one-year lease was signed with Dayspring Church prior to the June council meeting so they could complete their application for separate incorporation in Maryland. Nobody wanted to consider selling Dayspring, so that was never a comparable issue. Nevertheless, some Seekers felt outmaneuvered.

The council was also informed that a new church, The Church of the Servant Jesus, was emerging at 2025. Its mission was to support the ecumenical service and nurture new churches into being. It clearly had Gordon's blessing, and seemed to be a sign that he actually wanted to birth more little churches rather than ending Church of the Saviour. The new church would not be represented on the council because of the decision taken in January that no new churches would be added. The Church of the Servant Jesus never grew much larger than the three founding members, but it did take over stewardship of 2025 for several years.

On September 17, 1995, another C of S congregational meeting was held to debate the future of 2025. The meeting was billed as an opportunity to hear from anyone with a position on one of these three options:

a. Now is the time to sell 2025;

b. Now is the time to establish a long-term arrangement for 2025 with Seekers;

c. Now is the time to embrace a 3-year interim period with review at the end for 2025.

At that meeting, we also learned that Elizabeth O'Connor would stop working at 2025 on September 30. She had developed a brain tumor and needed to conserve her energy. That gave extra impetus to the need for some kind of Medigap funding for the C of S staff, which was one of the possibilities from the sale of 2025. Even though Gordon opposed any kind of a trust fund, others saw that the C of S staff had served long and faithfully on a minimal salary, and many people were concerned by the news that Elizabeth O'Connor's health was failing. The tide seemed to be turning toward selling 2025.

After the September congregational meeting and before the decisive October meeting, Sonya gave one of her rare sermons at Seekers. It was a ringing call to pick up our lives and walk! She called it "Pioneering

Disciples." Although Sonya had always been the champion of individual call, this time she challenged all Seekers to stand together and take collective action. She claimed *art* and *advocacy* as the charisms of Seekers. She made her vision for remaining a coherent committed body clear and strong: "The time for departure has arrived, the wagons are ready to move, disciples are gathering, baggage has been repacked, good-byes have been said. Let's move out!"

On October 5, 1995, another C of S congregational meeting was held to make a final decision on the future of 2025. Two votes were actually taken that day. In the first, 66 percent of those gathered voted to retain 2025 rather than sell. But then another vote was taken to retain the building only for a three-year interim period, ruling out Seekers' proposal for long-term stewardship.

That decision served to confirm Sonya's challenge and our energy shifted toward finding a new home. Those who had wanted to offer short-term stewardship fell silent and talk shifted to what we might be able to afford. Two weeks later, Celebration Circle inserted a brief commitment statement in the bulletin which slightly changed the open membership statement of 1991, deleting its reference to Church of the Saviour. It was a small declaration of independence from C of S, and the wording came from Celebration Circle, not the core members, but it definitely signaled our interpretation of the votes.[1]

CONNECTION WITH DAYSPRING

Since the beginning, Seekers had gathered for overnights at the Wellspring Center. The mood was generally light and playful, but this year Seekers carried a sense of being rejected by the other communities because of the decisions about 2025. Before the overnight, Brenda and Keith Seat requested an informal worship service to deposit the ashes of their daughter, Erica, in the Lake of the Saints. She had died at birth ten years earlier. Her twin, Marion, and their younger daughter, Lauren, would participate. I brought clay and, with the other children, we created a clay container that would dissolve in the lake along with her ashes. In a simple ritual that included the children, we installed a curved stone bench near the Wellspring Center, then walked down to the lake, where Peter and Sonya led us in a simple service. Committal of Erica's ashes into the Lake of the Saints was a sign

1. Appendix 7.

that Seekers would be rooted at Dayspring no matter what happened to the headquarters building in the city. The following month, on Seekers' silent retreat, Keith took a late afternoon photo of two geese that were nesting at the place where Erica's ashes were launched. An enlargement of Keith's photo is hanging in the Seekers library to commemorate the ritual—a sign of the Spirit's presence with us.

As 1995 came to an end, Mollie McMurray and Pat Conover called the "Homemakers" mission group, dedicated to finding a new home for Seekers. The C of S decision to delay sale of 2025 for three years gave us some time to do the inner and outer work necessary for the community to move out together. How that might happen, and when, would be led by the Spirit.

10

Holding the Tension
Letting the Creative Process Work

As THE NEW YEAR began, there was a sense of relief and clarity that Seekers would be moving out of 2025 when we could find a new home. It was a time to gather ourselves, look freshly at our common purpose, and assess our resources, both spiritual and financial. There was more attention to themes of art and advocacy in worship because of Sonya's sermon, and a focus on basic beliefs at the School of Christian Living. The community divided naturally into those who wanted to look for new space (outer journey) and those who were more concerned about the body of Seekers staying together (inner journey). In fact, we held the tension in community and did both as we entered a more relational period, in which we had to deepen our connections and trust the Spirit more.

A FUTURE FUND

Money was one place where both the inner journey advocates and scouts for a new home could join hands. In order to accumulate a down payment for new worship space, core members agreed to designate the money we had put into the Manna Capstone Fund over the years as the start of a future fund. Although still committed to giving away half of our contributed income beyond rent in any given year, we agreed to hold our external giving steady from then on, to keep our expenses down, and to place any net income into the Future Fund account rather than giving it away.

The budget for 1996 was set at $162,000, a new high for Seekers. The checkbook and record keeping were computerized for the first time, and the Financial Oversight Group (FOG) was formed to plan and oversee expenditures. FOG began meeting to make recommendations about the budget and cash flow as Bill Branner, the financial officer for Church of the Saviour, turned over pay records for the leadership team to Seekers. It was another step toward independence.

Once we incorporated separately from Church of the Saviour, Jeffrey Silverstone, the spouse of a core member, started a web page for Seekers to give us a presence in cyberspace. It was part of his personal website until the year 2000, when members allocated money to establish a separate site and confirmed him as our webmaster. He put some of our core documents, *The Guide to Seekers Church* and *The Mission Group Guide*, on the website for reference, and he regularly asked preachers to post their sermons. He also began posting the liturgies written by Celebration Circle and some of the prayers written by Sonya and Peter. The website was an invitation to greater articulation for an already wordy congregation, and all of us became more conscious that others would be able to read what we were saying to the community. Suddenly the intimacy of Seekers seemed to have glass walls.

Another effort to explore our future as a Spirit-led congregation was the Growing Edge Fund. As we gathered ourselves to become a more independent church in a new location, Sonya and Liz preached a sermon on the Growing Edge Fund. Sonya had identified *art* and *advocacy* as the core tenets of Seekers in her 1995 sermon, and she saw the fund as an important way to further that identity. As an artist herself, Liz had lived the path that she was inviting others to explore. "Creativity requires structure and limits," Liz said, "Some of the creativity is directly related to the church but other creativity does not seem to be.... It is through the individual creativity and faith journey that our collective candle of faith is reignited."

Sonya saw the possibilities for developing call not only in the recipients of Growing Edge Funds but in the partner who would walk with the recipient. She understood the charism of Seekers to be expressed in "creating the new." Companioning one another in those transfiguring experiences inspired many at Seekers. It could happen in mission groups. More likely, one would find another with a special interest in some new call, and would informally agree to be a prayer partner for that venture. The problem was that the desired "advocates" or "partners" were not always available, but the Growing Edge Fund continued to call forth new ventures and new partners who were willing to pray aloud for that person in worship, to nudge, ask questions, and encourage during the process.

Holding the Tension

In 1994, Roy Barber was given a Growing Edge grant to travel to Johannesburg, South Africa. Roy's mother had been active in the American civil rights movement, and Roy was drawn to the South African freedom movement. As a musician and teacher, Roy wanted to know whether he might feel a call to help in some way with creative drama. When he went, Nelson Mandela had been released from prison and had just been elected the first black president of South Africa. Seekers felt our support for Roy was one way of aiding the struggle for unity and peaceful transition.

Two years later, another group of Seekers made our first mission trip to El Salvador. From his position with the InterAmerican Foundation, Ron Arms made a connection for us with Dr. Vicky Guzman, a healthcare provider in the northern part of El Salvador. We had a class in the School of Christian Living for potential participants, and then nine Seekers, including two teens, embarked on a ten-day pilgrimage that included work with healthcare educators, microenterprise, and evening reflection together. The trip opened vistas on the world for all of us, and gave Seekers a specific connection for international giving in Central America like the one we were developing with South Africa.

ORDINATION AND INCLUSION

Once we incorporated separately, the question of whether core membership meant ordination arose again. At Church of the Saviour, the question of who could serve at the Communion table never came up because Gordon always presided, but for Seekers, determining our theology of ordination took on new urgency as regular attenders pressed for greater leadership. As a member of Celebration Circle, Deborah Sokolove circulated a paper titled "Considering Communion at Seekers." Although developed with a working group from Celebration Circle, the paper revealed Deborah's growing interest in theology, which would eventually lead her to Wesley Theological Seminary and ultimately to a doctorate in liturgical studies from Drew University. While supportive of leadership within the areas of call and mission group life, core members decided to retain the practice of allowing only core members to bless the elements for Communion.

But the function and powers of core members continued to trouble us. Questions of where to move, whether to rent or buy property, and who would make those decisions raised the issue of decision-making in Seekers. When we invited a former member of Seekers to facilitate a meeting on the purpose and structure of members' meetings, differences over decision-making quickly surfaced. Some people really valued time in the monthly core members' meeting for sharing, community building, and spiritual nourishment, while others felt those needs were met in their mission groups. It was another way of asking how serious we were about seeking the Spirit's guidance together. In the end, we agreed that community and spiritual nourishment needed to take place in our mission groups and that, during this stressful time of finding a new home, core member meetings would be primarily for keeping one another informed and involved. In essence, we decided to take an administrative path rather than a more relational approach.

TO BUY OR NOT TO BUY

The Homemakers mission group worked hard to find Seekers a new home in the District, on the Metro, with play space for children. They identified about one hundred available buildings, of which forty were worth reviewing. They also explored sharing space with two downtown churches. Both had traditional worship spaces and, as we looked into those spaces, we agreed that we wanted a more flexible space with movable chairs. When they had narrowed the choices, Homemakers sponsored a day trip to look at five different buildings and used the feedback on safety, location, and types of space to prioritize the guidelines for their search. They also eliminated commercial leasing (too expensive) and buying land to build on (no suitable plots). Informally, we began to focus on finding a distressed building to renovate.

The 1997 budget was set for a 15 percent increase, an enormous stretch at a time we did not seem to be growing in numbers. For the first time, the budget included a line item for a future location, along with an agreement not to fund it, rather than reducing our giving if we did not, in fact, reach our ambitious budget goal. However, some members voiced their suspicion that we would fund that first if we found a building to buy.

When Homemakers identified two potential commercial buildings for sale, all Seekers were invited to visit the sites and imagine ourselves there. There was a congregational meeting to discuss those possibilities and we put a contingency contract on a vacant print plant at 1101 Pennsylvania Avenue SE to hold it until the community could make a decision. In response, Ron Arms wrote a spirited letter to the core members opposing the

Holding the Tension

purchase of *any* building, along with his position of opposing paid leadership, supporting open membership, and reminding us that Seekers believed in the priesthood of all believers. Ron's experience as a pastor suggested to him that a building and paid staff would automatically take the bulk of the budget and diminish external giving.

Seekers had a full congregational meeting, which the core members promised to take as guidance on whether to make an offer to buy the vacant commercial space on Pennsylvania Avenue. When a straw vote was taken, 47 percent of those gathered were "eager to proceed," 28 percent agreed we should go ahead and make a bid, but 25 percent were firmly opposed. That evening, core members spent a great deal of time discussing Ron's letter, considering factors of spirit, call, and place before taking a vote on whether to proceed with a contingency contract. Some people objected to the location, others to the neighborhood (which was perceived to be anti-gay), and others to the lack of play space for children. Underneath it all was the fear that the decision would split Seekers into factions, and we wanted to hold the community together. In the end, only two thirds of the twenty-four core members favored purchase, so we did *not* go ahead.

Disappointed in the outcome, Pat and Mollie "set down" their call to be the Homemakers mission group, although they continued to look for space informally.

MEMBERS REGROUP

In response to the decision not to buy the Pennsylvania Avenue property, Learners & Teachers sponsored a series of summer discussions on Tuesday nights, based on the four classes (belonging, decision-making, stewardship, and space) that had drawn Seekers to the school just after the vote to disband Church of the Saviour. Even though Seekers did have a general membership statement, some people still felt the need for a greater sense of belonging and influence without being a core member. Ron was particularly vocal about that, but others who felt they could not tithe or commit to a mission group were equally adamant about wanting their say in where Seekers would be located.

Sonya also did her best to keep the core group from polarizing for or against purchase of a building. She heard the talk about splitting into a Virginia church and a Maryland church as a threat, and in her usual inclusive way she held up our common commitment as the larger value. She led core members in a discussion about our commitment to be a community together and emphasized these values: "We are called by Christ to a shared life, joined to each other for better or for worse in unlimited liability, our purpose is to build on one another's gifts for common good." As a relational strategy for holding the tensions among us, Sonya's approach was effective and invitational.

JUBILEE CELEBRATION

On October 19, 1997, a huge crowd gathered in a striped tent at Dayspring to celebrate the Jubilee (fifty years) of Church of the Saviour. Obviously it had not disbanded or disappeared, in spite of the vote to do so. There were thirteen churches listed in the program, although only nine were incorporated as co-owners of Dayspring. Each of the churches submitted a brief statement of its call for the bulletin and all were represented in the program.

Shortly after the Jubilee celebration, the C of S council received a letter from Gordon and Mary Cosby requesting that the council *not* move to sell 2025 for another three years, until September 2000. The letter also noted that the Church of the Servant Jesus would be taking official responsibility for the building instead of Seekers. On October 26 the C of S council approved their request and decided that "proceeds from the sale of 2025 would be divided evenly among the churches existing as part of CoS as of November, 1994, and still in existence when the property is sold." Council minutes also noted that Christ House was dissolving as a church, a decision that removed it from a share of the proceeds.

The Cosbys' request for an extension gave Seekers another three years to find a new home and the promise of a share of the sale of 2025. Peter, who had been overseeing maintenance of 2025, supplied the council with a list of needed repairs as Seekers drew back from becoming the steward of 2025. Then little things began to make 2025 feel less like home for us. Doors were locked. Dishes sequestered. Cabinets marked for special purposes. Although nothing was said specifically, Seekers felt we were being encouraged to leave. In retrospect, these were helpful in getting the community motivated to move, but at the time it felt like we were being ushered out the door.

EVOKING A VISION

After resting for six months following the decision not to purchase the property on Pennsylvania Avenue, we began to gather energy for another attempt. The leadership team sought to build a sense of common purpose among the twenty-one core members by asking them to write out their answers to these questions:

1. Church. As a do-it-yourself church, we are becoming . . .

2. Community. As a small group, scattered around the city, we are becoming . . .

3. Ministry. As busy, committed people, our call to ministry is . . .

4. Growth. We want some room for growth and new initiatives. I want Seekers to have more . . .

5. Grounded (in faith) and empowered to be loving and doing God's will. For me, that means more . . .

6. Living in God's story. For me, emerging signs of this connection . . .

The exercise was intended to evoke new energy for the move among core members, who would presumably be providing most of the money needed to purchase a building. We wanted to discern the call of the Holy Spirit, be practical, and involve as many Seekers as possible, but we recognized that consensus was probably not feasible, so we decided that a specific choice to move ahead would require only 75 percent of the twenty-one core members, because the pressure to make a decision was increasing as time went on.

Acknowledging the limits of having a mission group look for space, another group was authorized by core members to develop specific recommendations for new space. This time, no attempt would be made to practice the spiritual disciplines of a mission group because of its limited focus. Meetings and membership would be open at all times, and the charge would simply be to "find Seekers a new home." The Space/Location Task Force would look at buying, renting, or even building a home for Seekers.

Since the abandoned print shop at 1101 Pennsylvania Avenue SE was still available, the task force was urged to look at that property again, even though a strong segment of the core members had turned it down the first time because of its location and lack of play space for children. Volunteers for the task force agreed to work at keeping the wider congregation appraised of its work by posting a large map upstairs, marking potential sites, and inviting people to their biweekly meetings.

Sonya's identification of *art* and *advocacy* as the essence of Seekers surfaced again when Roy Barber asked Seekers to sponsor a group of South African youth for a month-long fundraising trip to the US. He had used a small inheritance from his mother to purchase tickets for this first group from Winterveldt. They would be performing Roy's play, *The Gift*, in a variety of places to raise money for educating a wider group of at-risk youth who were connected with the Bokamoso Youth Center. Sonya and Manning hosted one of the young women for two weeks; others opened their homes as well. There was much excitement when they performed a shortened version of the play at worship, and there was some talk of a return visit by some in the Artists group to South Africa. Imagining a new home for Seekers that would be hospitable for music and theater performances then became part of our search for a new home.

URGENCY INCREASES

Elizabeth O'Connor died on October 17, 1998, at the age of seventy-seven. Her prophetic writing had been a guide and inspiration for so many people, near and far. Her death seemed to loosen the hold that 2025 had for some of the older members of Seekers, and we became more aware that most of the newer members had no direct experience of the original church, even though we were still gathering for Sunday worship in the headquarters building at 2025.

For Seekers, Manning Dyer's mobility was becoming more of a problem because of his Parkinson's disease, and the search for new space took on more urgency as we wondered how long he would be able to use the stairs. The task force reported that they were ready once again to engage an agent with these criteria: Metro access, play space for children, acquisition cost no higher than $1.2 million, and worship space of 1,200 square feet—about what we had at 2025. Those parameters became the guidelines, even though we had not figured out how we might raise such a large sum of money.

Holding the Tension

Since the decision by C of S members not to have Seekers take on stewardship of 2025, giving had risen about 7 percent each year, while FOG kept our expenditures down and external giving at the same level. Although that would not give us a million dollars in the near future, it did suggest that we could have a significant down payment in the Future Fund when added to the amount we had loaned to Manna.

The Space/Location Task Force became the New Home Task Force (NHTF) as 1999 began. The name change essentially ended their search for shared space or rental space, and signaled to the rest of the congregation that we would buy or build a home of our own. Numerous task groups formed for specific purposes in the next few years, giving newcomers who were not yet in mission groups a chance to participate where they could. In addition to their mission group responsibilities, core members were also involved in these task groups, which meant they were carrying even more responsibility during this time of transition. As a whole, we seemed glad to grant decision-making authority at the point of those interests without requiring the disciplines of a mission group.

Soon after forming, the NHTF scheduled a community visit to 276 Carroll Street NW as a potential site for Seekers. This derelict property was a sad-looking combination of a hundred-year-old house and a fifty-year-old storefront office building across from a Metro stop at the northernmost tip of the District, adjacent to Takoma Park, Maryland. It was on the market for $345,000, an amount we could pay with our Future Fund, although it would leave us nothing for renovations.

When the whole community met for an open discussion about the Carroll Street property, there was considerable concern about the "elders" living in Virginia because of the increased driving distance from the Dupont Circle location of 2025. There was still some interest in dividing the community into two house churches, one in Virginia and one in Maryland, but the strongest sense of the meeting was to stay together and take whatever pruning would result if we moved to the northern edge of the District. In a memo dated January 31, 1999, the NHTF voted to propose purchase of the Carroll Street property. However, before the proposal could be considered, someone else made a bid on the property and it was taken off the market. It was another disappointment for those ready to buy!

INCLUDING EVERYONE

Meanwhile, another ad hoc group offered language to strengthen the general membership statement, which had been in the recommitment bulletin since 1991. The group wanted to retain the polity of a committed core group, but knew we would need the financial support of *all* Seekers in order to buy a building, so the question of how to include everyone in the decision with their sense of belonging was critically important. The ad hoc group also suggested a small addition to the core members' statement, stating that they would be "accountable for the organizational health of Seekers." It was a tiny addition with big implications for what might happen if we purchased a place that might be inaccessible for a number of current Seekers. Who would carry the financial burden? What constituted the "organizational health" of Seekers Church? If we moved to Maryland, who would care for those left behind in Virginia or vice versa? How would we make those decisions?

By the time a new commitment statement was ready for approval in 2001, we all agreed that the addition "to care for the organizational health of the community" was necessary, but there were still some who resisted that organizational aspect of core membership in favor of that group being the spiritual heart of Seekers. The report also raised the question of whether we should change the name of the core members group to Stewards, but we could not agree on a new name because we were still not in agreement about their fundamental role.[1]

Pressured by the search for new space and questions about who had the authority to make those decisions in Seekers, Pat circulated a paper on "Membership and Decision-Making in Seekers." In it he addressed the *intentionality* he hoped all members would have about claiming a specific path of spiritual growth. He made a case for retaining a committed core group accountable for the health of the whole community, and warned core members against relinquishing the authority to make binding decisions for the community, even as he recognized the awkward slowness of decision-making at our monthly meetings. He was particularly leery of letting the "paid staff" make decisions, even though nobody was suggesting that. Others wanted the whole congregation to make decisions.

Preaching that summer focused on authority and commitment, while we all tried to hold the energy of staying at 2025 and finding a new home at

---

1. Appendix 5.

the same time. As a result of this creative tension, core members agreed to change their title to "Stewards" as an accurate expression of our function in Seekers, so anyone who wanted to make a declaration of intentional growth could become a member of Seekers.

TIME TO BUY?

Amid all the hoopla and fears about the year 2000, and what would happen to our computer-driven society, many Seekers gathered for a vigil at the home of John and Kay Schultz in Burkittsville, Maryland, to welcome the new millennium together. After a worship service in which we cast old things into a huge bonfire, we quietly gathered inside to name our hopes for the future. Once again, we were actively stalking the Spirit, seeking guidance for a clear path together as we searched for a new home. That night, we also had a sense that the Spirit was stalking us, leaving signs and hints of the direction we were to take together.

The new millennium began with the news that the Carroll Street property was again on the market. The New Home Task Force exercised their authority to put down a contingency contract and suddenly it seemed that we would be moving out of 2025 in the near future. At the next C of S council meeting, Kate announced that Seekers would be deciding whether to proceed with the purchase, and she also informed them that Sonya would be leaving the staff of Seekers in June. At that same meeting, in response to another request from Gordon, the sale of 2025 was put off another two years. That was good news to us, because Seekers would have a place to worship as we faced the prospect of choosing new leadership, new forms of membership, and maybe having a derelict building to renovate.

In an effort to listen more intently for the Holy Spirit's guidance, Jesse Palidofsky, a hospice chaplain at Holy Cross Hospital, called for an all-Seekers retreat at Rolling Ridge on the last weekend of January. Jesse brought his Quaker experience of listening for guidance to the momentous questions before us. To support Jesse's initiative, another Seeker with a Quaker background provided the fee to bring Suzanne Farnham of *Listening Hearts* to lead the Rolling Ridge retreat. Most Seekers attended, even though busy schedules had to be adjusted quickly in order to be there. It was a time of guided listening, contemplative conversation, and creative dreaming together. In the end, there was a general consensus that it was time to move ahead toward purchase of the building.

Stalking the Spirit

For a community where feelings matter, it was particularly hard to hear the vigorous dissent of Ron Arms, who had just become a Steward the month before this retreat. Citing the burden of ownership on our ability to give freely, and the distance of 276 Carroll Street from Virginia residents, he noted how the Future Fund was already holding down increases in our external giving. To reconcile those objections, Brenda Seat offered this statement for approval by Stewards:

> Seekers church will purchase the property on Carroll Street as our new home. We see this place as both an opportunity for mission and a home for the community life of Seekers. We affirm our commitment to spend as much on mission as we do on Seekers and will work to maintain an equilibrium between resources offered for each. *We intend to do this by increasing resources budgeted for mission until we restore this equilibrium and pledging to pay mission commitments as a first priority.*

However, after much discussion, the last sentence was deleted out of fear that we simply could not do it if we purchased a building. It was a tacit agreement that Ron's dissident voice was probably right about the financial burden of owning a building. Ron stood aside from the vote, and the core members unanimously adopted a resolution to authorize the purchase of 276 Carroll Street NW for $345,000 on February 5, 2000.

At first, there was a sense that we would be moving very soon. We blithely assumed that bringing the building up to code, and installing an elevator, would be a simple and straightforward process. Along with planning for the move to Carroll Street, we knew that Sonya and Manning would be moving to North Carolina in August, where Manning could get help with his Parkinson's disease and they could be closer to their grandchildren.

With Sonya leaving, Celebration Circle decided to open the liturgist's role to any woman in CC when a man was preaching, and the two other men in CC would share the liturgist's role with Peter when a woman was preaching. Generally the transition was welcomed as a sign that Sonya's departure would create space for new voices to emerge, although some felt that having more liturgists would destabilize the prayerful part of our worship.

Soon after Sonya left, the Hope and a Home mission group disbanded, leaving Kate Cudlipp, chair of the FLOC (For Love of Children) board, as our only remaining connection to FLOC. According to Cynthia Dahlin, who had been a member of that group, Hope and a Home volunteers were increasingly excluded from information about the families they were supporting as the paid staff as FLOC became more professional. Although they had tried to create a situation where paid and unpaid staff could work together, it wasn't successful. Once Sonya left, the group set down their call and the mission group members looked for new places of belonging and service within Seekers.

11

New Leadership Emerges
Transition to the Next Generation at Seekers

IN 2000, THE NUMBER of Stewards grew to a peak of twenty-six and enthusiasm for moving to our new place was high, especially among the newer members who lived on the north side of the District or in Maryland. In the two months after our decision to buy the building on Carroll Street, there were four community meetings, and ten working groups formed to focus on different aspects of the move and renovation. Although everyone was already overcommitted, finding time and energy for these meetings suddenly seemed possible.

Renovating the space and developing new leadership were much more difficult than we could have imagined. To mobilize the Stewards, our leadership team, Kate Cudlipp and Peter Bankson, invited all Stewards to engage with these questions:

1. How might we transmit our values to new people unfamiliar with Church of the Saviour?

2. What would be the optimum size for Seekers?

3. Were people going to burn out by serving on committees rather than joining a mission group?

4. What about ongoing efforts for Sunday school and silent retreat?

5. What about organizational and emotional issues around Sonya's departure?

New Leadership Emerges

6. Did Stewards need a "spiritual director" for this period?

7. How might we ground this transition process more spiritually?

There were no simple answers to those questions, although the questions describe the range of concerns that Peter and Kate were aware of.

In response to those questions, Stewards began to think about how to select someone new for the leadership team. We were hopefully naive about what it would take to develop new leadership and move to a new building.

MONEY FOR RENOVATION

After purchase of the building, our attention turned to the question of how to finance a renovation. Through a combination of gifts and cash on hand, we had purchased the building outright, but it was clear that considerable reconstruction would be needed to even bring the building up to code for use as a church. A temporary stewardship group gathered to brainstorm ideas for preparing the community to undertake the financial challenge of raising about $600,000, which we thought would be what was needed for renovations.

We started with a two-step process: to ask Seekers and former Seekers to consider one-time gifts for the renovation, as well as increasing their regular giving. Then later we would ask for loans. We drew on the tradition of generosity that had been a thread in Seekers from the beginning, and began with several sermons about giving from our total wealth rather than just a tithe of current income.

The stewardship group gave the following questions to all current members of Seekers, and they also included them in a letter to former members who might be interested in supporting our future location:

1. What are the issues I need to work on in order to give to Seekers from a sense of freedom and joy rather than obligation?

2. Do I feel any guilt about the way I manage my income and wealth? What is the source of such guilt and what do I need to do to release it?

3. Do I manage my income and wealth in a way that acknowledges that God has priority in my life? Where, in addition to Seekers, is that reflected?

4. In giving to Seekers, do I need to work with issues of trying to buy approval? Am I merely responding to some sense of a common standard?

5. Would increased giving to Seekers, in a one-time gift or through weekly or monthly offerings, enhance my feeling of solidarity with the community; of being invested in the future of Seekers?

The response was nothing short of amazing! By October of 2000 we had $247,320 in outright gifts and $659,000 in promised loans from forty people. That meant nearly everybody in the congregation would have a financial stake in the renovation.

A Building Development Team (BDT) was formed to monitor the renovation. Keith Seat, a lawyer and professional mediator, volunteered to chair that group. Glen Yakushiji brought his expertise in sound and lighting equipment. Deborah Sokolove added her aesthetic sensibility, and Peter brought his practical design skills. Together, they began working on a plan for the renovation with Sara Woodhead, a local architect, who was interested in renovating old buildings in Washington, DC. Other joined them for certain phases of the work, but those four really carried the responsibility of overseeing the renovation for us.

Deciding on details of the renovation began in earnest. Nobody wanted space that would be dark and dingy, or unfit to be used for new calls that might emerge, but in the wake of Sonya's departure, fears about our future as a community were also high. Brenda Seat held out a positive vision of new missions that might develop from the building, urging the BDT to trust that additional costs could be absorbed. Some were hesitant about Brenda's generous spirit and her obvious delight in celebration and hospitality, but we also needed such hopeful leadership to carry the project to completion. Others worried that the building would undercut outreach giving from the Seekers budget.

Only those on the BDT knew the complexity and cost beginning to unfold as plans for the renovation were being discussed. Deborah and Peter were particularly aware of how much the whole community needed to hear encouragement in worship, because they were directly involved in both the BDT and Celebration Circle. During that period, CC paid special attention to creating liturgies of hope and unity. When our spirits seemed to be flagging, Deborah preached a crucial sermon titled "Bread and Roses." In it, she called on Seekers to embrace both justice *and* beauty—to trust the BDT and to spend the money to make the building beautiful as well as functional. She included words from a song inspired by striking mill workers in Lawrence, Massachusetts, who wanted not only living wages as seamstresses or domestics, but the "small graces" that make life worth living: "Small art and love and beauty their drudging spirits knew. Yes, it is bread we fight for, but we fight for roses too."[1]

Deborah's sermon seemed to shift the mood at Seekers, making us more confident that we could raise the money that we needed for renovation without undercutting our operating budget. In particular, Stewards wanted to keep the spirit of generosity and outreach as a hallmark of Seekers. Although Stewards had decided not to raise the level of external giving to match anticipated increases in contributed income, we promised ourselves that we would not lower outreach giving either.

As the millennium year ended, there was a sense of guarded optimism and hopefulness about our new space and new initiatives that seemed to be emerging in the wake of Sonya's departure. The liturgy for the Advent season was designed to celebrate our diversity yet give us a sense of being woven together into a single creative circle, a sign of our life as a called community. The theme for Advent was "A Bright Snarl." On the altar, a soft, shiny tangle of many different yarns, roving and sparkling threads, spoke of the different strands in our community. It became the Advent wreath, encircling four large candles. The bulletin cover was a rich lavender color with biblical text wound like yarn on the surface, which looked like a curving path toward the future.

Once again Celebration Circle helped us envision a brighter snarl of life to which God was calling us as a community. As though to confirm our intention to be generous with our money, we decided to allocate the special Christmas offering (about $3,000) to Wellspring for a handicapped room at the lodge, to New Community Church for their after-school program, and to the Faithful Servant Trust Fund.

MEN STEP FORWARD

Several men stepped forward in the wake of Sonya's departure. After years of quiet cooperation with the feminist leaders at Seekers, the men seemed confident and ready for a new form of partnership with the women as a more relational period began to emerge. On New Year's Day 2001, Kevin Ogle invited Seekers to a memorial service for his father, who had died ten

---

1. September 17, 2000.

years before, while estranged from his family. Kevin had connected with his "father wound" during a class at the School of Christian Living, and had the courage to ask Seekers for a memorial service, to which he invited his mother. As a therapist himself, it was an act of faith and trust in the community for him to ask for this ritual. The sanctuary was full that day. I suspect we were also grieving Sonya's departure in a substitutionary memorial, however unconscious that was.

Jesse Palidofsky and Kevin drew many of the men in Seekers for a winter class called "Joyfully Masculine," and they joined Billy Amoss and Peter from CC to lead one of the first men's retreats at Rolling Ridge. Glen Yakushiji and Jesse began to offer monthly sing-alongs for anyone who wanted to participate in order to encourage congregational singing as a unifying practice. Since then, Glen has continued these informal sing-alongs, alternating host sites in Maryland, the District, and Virginia, to encourage home visits that are open to any Seeker as another way to build community among our geographically scattered members.

Peter continued to partner with Kate Cudlipp on the Seekers' leadership team, and other men shouldered major responsibilities for the building renovation. Glen made sure we had a performance-grade sound and light system in the new building, and Jeffrey Silverstone expanded Seekers' presence on the web. After so much turmoil and indecision about moving, their leadership emerged just when we needed it most.

RESTATING OUR VALUES

Defining our interior life also took on new importance as we looked toward republishing the *Guide to Seekers Church* for the new location. Discussion of what general membership in Seekers meant provided Stewards with yet another opportunity to consider the language of spiritual leadership without Sonya's guiding hand.

Describing the inner life of the community was both stimulating for some of the newer members and tedious for others who thought those issues had been described well enough. David Lloyd raised his concerns that Seekers seemed more focused on inclusion and belonging, rather than commitment and discipline. In response to David's concerns, other Stewards recognized the danger of idolizing community, but affirmed our intention to honor the spiritual journeys of those who wanted to be members but not Stewards. Brenda was vocal about her belief that making a commitment to community often creates the conditions for faith to blossom, and that identifying with *lived truth* often comes before making a more abstract public commitment to that truth.

Intense discussion was a primary way of holding the tension between inclusion and commitment, embracing more open membership and preserving a committed core. By fall, the recommitment group was ready with a new statement of general membership. In addition to this commitment for all members, Stewards changed their own commitment statement by adding the following responsibilities:

- Care for the whole of creation, beginning with the natural environment;
- Take responsibility for the organizational health of Seekers Church.[2]

That it took so long to make these few changes could be seen as laziness or stubbornness on the part of Stewards, but with the addition of five new Stewards in the previous two years, discussions about belonging and commitment served as a way to include them in defining the primary values of Seekers.

RENOVATION GLITCH

The first major glitch in our renovation process came when the architect took another job with the District of Columbia. She arranged for the BDT to meet with her boss in hope that he would continue the renovation project on schedule, but we could see signs of trouble in the transition. Then Keith brought the bad news that the lowest bid on our project had come in at $1.5 million, about 75 percent higher than the architect's estimate. Stewards decided to wait and see if there were others who might be interested in bidding on our renovation job. Their willingness to wait seemed Spirit-led.

Meanwhile, Keith, Peter, and Pat worked on a protocol for soliciting more loans. When the loan group presented these guidelines to Stewards, the congregation was down to about fifty adults (including the twenty-six Stewards) and a dozen children. We wanted to borrow the money for renovation from ourselves as another way of getting everyone to invest in the process. During the recommitment season, these guidelines for renovation

2. Appendix 5.

loans were shared with the congregation and alumni in other parts of the country:

1. Loans would be made in increments of $1,000;
2. The term could be open-ended or repayment specified;
3. Seekers reserves the right to repay ahead of schedule;
4. If repayment is needed early, Seekers will make every effort to provide that within 30 days;
5. Lender may specify interest rates from zero to 8%;
6. Interest on non-zero loans will be paid annually.

After several sermons and another class in the school on the spiritual aspect of money, we had $58,900 in new gifts, bringing the cash on hand total to $408,000. In addition, twenty-four loans were actually made (out of the forty which had been promised earlier) for a total of $810,000, with an average interest rate of 5 percent. That brought the total available to $1.218 million—just what we thought would be needed. Then the BDT concluded a contract with Providence Construction, a for-profit arm of Manna, which we had been supporting for years. Finally the reconstruction of 276 Carroll Street was ready to begin!

BEST PRACTICES

In 2001, Seekers was selected as one of nine congregations chosen for a book by Paul Wilkes, titled *Excellent Protestant Congregations*. As one of the people interviewed for this project, I was then invited to represent Seekers at a pastoral summit in New Orleans. Funded by the Lily Foundation, the summit was an eclectic gathering of carefully selected Catholic and Protestant churches, each presenting their "best practices." Being a lay-led church made us unique, and I was scheduled to lead three different workshops to explain how Seekers handled education, spiritual formation, and worship without clergy direction.

During the discussion time in those three workshops, Pat and Peter presented other aspects of Seekers as well, but in the end we felt that Seekers' form of shared leadership seemed to be quite beyond the ken of those clergy-led congregations. When the book from the summit, *Best Practices*

New Leadership Emerges

from America's Best Churches, finally came out in 2003, my chapter on Seekers was titled "The Power of Commitment: It Can Happen Anywhere." Just then, however, we weren't so sure.

Within the wider Church of the Saviour community, Tom and Carolyn Hubers sent a letter to the C of S churches and individual "graduates" near and far, requesting financial support for a new effort to link the various ministries that had grown out of C of S. They wanted to establish a newspaper called *The Diaspora*, which would be published quarterly and sent to anyone who asked for a copy. They felt that the churches and separately incorporated ministries were losing touch with their C of S heritage, and wanted the newspaper to give some visibility to the wider network. Stewards allocated some funds and Muriel volunteered to be our regular correspondent. She had long advocated for more connection among the churches, and this seemed like a step in that direction.

STAFF OR LEADERSHIP?

In July of 2001, Jeanne Marcus sent an email to Peter and Kate indicating that she was feeling a call to "the leadership team" at Seekers. Even though the practice had been to wait until Stewards issued an invitation for someone to join the staff, Jeanne wanted to name her own call and ask the community to confirm it. How to do that was a question without precedent. Peter and Kate responded to Jeanne's query by requesting Stewards to set up a "staff needs discernment group." They clearly saw themselves as staff, not leaders or decision-makers in the traditional sense.

In response, and with a certain lightness of being, Jeanne and two other women offered a month-long class on "The Shadow in Seekers." Most of the women in Seekers signed up, but the men did not. Out of that shadow class, most of the Seekers women came to a pre-wedding shower as our "shadow selves"—a hilarious display of our hidden "gifts." Underneath, however, I think there was a need for the women of Seekers to join hands to feel our strength now that Sonya's voice was gone. Whether the energy in our shadow selves could be made more conscious was another question.

Jeanne asked that her call be considered separately from the discernment of staffing needs, but Stewards were reluctant to do that. During the discussion of Jeanne's call, there was a consistent use of the word "staff" rather than "leadership team." Pat was particularly strong about rejecting the notion of a leadership team, although he seemed satisfied with the administrative and coordinating function that Peter and Kate had been offering. Because both of them had been in government service for many years, both seemed comfortable with the organizational role they had assumed for Stewards and for Seekers. Neither one claimed special gifts for pastoring or prophetic preaching, although I believe there was an unspoken assumption by many Stewards that the staff team would continue to nurture, care for, and guide members of Seekers who were not in mission groups. That need spoke to Jeanne, calling forth her gifts and experience as a lawyer and community organizer.

Just then, on September 11, 2001, the twin towers of the World Trade Center in New York and the Pentagon in Washington, DC, were hit by terrorists. David was directly affected by the Pentagon disaster because he worked for the Defense Department and knew people who died there. We all felt our helplessness and need for someone, anyone, who could be a good pastor or a good shepherd. On the following Sunday, we gathered in silence for most of the service. We needed to be together, to claim God's presence as our deeper security in the chaotic world. The special offering for Afghan relief that day gathered the startling amount of $4,450 over and above our usual giving.

In the wake of the 9/11 disaster, Stewards revisited the question of Jeanne's call to the leadership team. Although Jeanne had offered to work two days a week, Stewards decided that if the community confirmed her call she would be added at one day a week for a year, while the slower process of discerning our leadership needs for the move and resettlement took place. At that time, Kate was being paid for two days a week and Peter, who was still working at Communities in Schools, was paid for one day a week. In addition, both volunteered their time for mission group activities. Adding Jeanne would give us four days of compensated staff time.

A new Staff Needs Discernment Group (SNDG) was formed. The name signaled the mindset of most Stewards—that we needed administrative help, not spiritual guidance. Pat sent an email to all Stewards regarding his position on "paying for help in Seekers." He began by saying that it was critical to him that the responsibility for guiding Seekers resides with Stewards rather than a "clergy leader." He named the break with that tradition when Fred left. "Now," he said, "Sonya has left and we must *not* try to replace her."

The SNDG identified pastoring as a special gift that Sonya had brought to Seekers, especially for members outside of the mission group structures.

Pat's email said that we hired Jeanne in response to statements of need by Peter and Kate "for more help with the work of listening, connecting, encouraging, and general enabling and coordination." In other words, we did need to replace Sonya's gifts for the work of pastoring the community.

The issue of how to listen to and care for people who were not in mission groups continued to bubble underneath our focus on renovating the Carroll Street building. Learners & Teachers helped by offering classes in the school that seemed to touch the emotional concerns of the wider community. There were classes on death and dying, dealing with conflict, doing *midrash* with biblical texts, and providing spiritual companionship. People seemed eager to participate, and the classes helped to deepen our sense of caring for each other in times of need as we waited for our new home. Then the SNDG set up meetings on the second and fourth Sundays of every month, open to any Seeker, to hammer out a description of our staff needs. For those of us who hate interminable meetings, it looked like a long winter indeed!

THE FUNCTIONS OF STEWARDS

As the question of having paid staff began to pick up energy, Stewards recognized the challenge in Pat's email (noted above) and took time to brainstorm the function of Stewards. Jeanne brought her skill and experience as a group facilitator, and she began to help Stewards look at how we might be organized more effectively. "If Stewards are the primary source of leadership and decision-making for the community," she said, "it is important for the group to understand that." The list of functions that we saw for ourselves was long and varied. Although awareness of pastoral functions was growing among Stewards, nobody claimed spiritual leadership for the community as an expectation of Stewards, and nobody named pastoring the community either. In the wake of Sonya's departure, we wondered how those gifts for spiritual leadership and pastoring would emerge.

Peter tried to address the differences between those Stewards who wanted more spiritual nurture and personal sharing in the meetings and those who thought we already had too little time for the business at hand. In preparation, he circulated a paper titled "The Stewards' Commitment and the Work We Do Together." He reminded us that Church of the Saviour had a simpler hierarchical structure than Seekers. The C of S staff took care of policy and administration, the council simply approved staff proposals, and core members rarely met as a single body. In contrast, Seekers had adopted the principle of shared leadership, beginning with Fred and Sonya's effort to build a strong core group to share in both visioning and administration. "In Seekers," he reminded us, "we ask Stewards to do it all." He did not describe any special role for the staff team.

Actually, the staff team, Kate, Peter, and Jeanne, had no particular visibility at Seekers. They weren't listed in the bulletin or on the website, and they didn't preach more often than others or direct any programs either. But Stewards depended on the staff team to listen for needs in the community, keep track of ongoing issues, and set the agenda for the monthly Stewards meetings. The staff team usually facilitated one segment or another, and, when needed, they planned a process that would help stewards reach a decision. The pastoring function of the staff team went largely unnoticed and unnamed, although when Sonya left we learned how important it was by the level of dissatisfaction that welled up.

In an effort to find a structure that would make space for those who wanted more relational time, and as well as for those who wanted to debate policy, Peter suggested we might identify "Mary Stewards" and "Martha Stewards," who would meet at the same time for different tasks, but there was no consensus to do that. At another meeting, Peter suggested that we might have a conscious discernment of gifts among Stewards, but there were other Stewards who did not believe that the process of confirming gifts should be done in Stewards, although it was done regularly in mission groups. Peter also suggested that we find a way to offer public recognition of the work that various members were doing as mission beyond the church. Stewards were again unable or unwilling to respond to Peter's initiatives. We seemed stuck and fearful about the challenges ahead.

Then a group of "spirit guides" formed to deepen our pastoring skills for the wider community. About fifteen key people, including Kate, Peter, and Jeanne, attended those monthly sessions. Most of the mission group spiritual directors and a few other potential guides came to learn practical ways to deepen the community's inner life. Because we were largely powerless to do anything about the speed, or lack of it, of readying the building for use, the Stewards kept working on ways to deepen connections with the wider community, even as we wrangled over our leadership needs. Most of the people in the spirit guides group were Stewards, which meant that they were also carrying weekly mission group responsibilities and monthly Stewards meetings as well.

New Leadership Emerges

Our concerns turned to celebration when two Stewards, Ken Burton and Jane Engle, were married in April 2002. Both Ken and Jane had strong interests in liturgy, so they designed their own wedding ceremony. Peter and Jeanne simply brought "blessings" from the community, but they didn't really officiate in a formal sense. There were statements of support from their families and friends, followed by dinner and dancing in the lovely ambience of the old mansion at 2025, brought to life by new love.

LEADERSHIP AND COMPENSATION

Finally, the Staff Needs Discernment Group was ready with recommendations about our needs for paid leadership. The report began by looking at our values as a community rooted in biblical faith, ecumenicity, and shared leadership. The report noted that Seekers believes in the "priesthood of all believers" but recognizes that there are certain priestly functions that require state licensing. The SNDG report addressed the charged issues of leadership and authority: "We struggled to find the words to name why compensation is important for the leadership team. We said it is a way of acknowledging the team's authority, but at the same time, we recognized that others in Seekers exercise leadership and are granted authority but are not paid."

Following this narrative explanation of their process, the SNDG made these specific recommendations, which were adopted by Stewards:

1. That the team be referred to as "the Leadership Team";

2. That we wanted the team to embody the values listed in our 1993 Call to Leadership of the Whole plus "Holding up or working with issues of marginalized people in our culture;"

3. That the team be three to five people working a total of seven days/week;

4. That we use the word "stipend" and budget for seven days/week with compensation levels based on experience and the amount of time an individual is willing to offer;

5. That team members should serve in staggered three-year terms. At the end of each 3-year term, a discernment process with a "leadership liaison group" will mutually determine further service;

6. That Stewards will issue an invitation to the Leadership Team and a Search team (of Stewards and Members) would seek a reasonable balance of gender representation on the leadership team. In addition, Stewards should acknowledge the validity of a process whereby persons come forward, as Jeanne Marcus did, out of their own sense of call, regardless of whether a formal invitation to the team is outstanding.

While many breathed a sigh of relief that we had finally identified what we wanted on the leadership team, one Steward, who had been on a leave of absence and had not participated in the SNDG, raised her concerns about the term "leadership team." Others also objected to the term "leadership team," calling on all Stewards to take the notion of servanthood more seriously.

Not able to reach consensus on the language of the SNDG report, a smaller group of Stewards agreed to rework the report. Of the new group, only Deborah had been a member of the SNDG over those long winter months, when they had solicited input over and over. There they had discussed the need for leadership, as well as the extra level of commitment the staff team needed to have, but the critics had not been part of those discussions and now they exercised their power to halt the process.

Displaced grief over Sonya's departure seemed to be part of the criticism. The critics also seemed to be reacting to talk by some of the men at Seekers that their dedication arose from commitment and duty, rather than a more feminine sense of "deep joy." For those who knew Sonya, it was easy to miss her cheerful enthusiasm, her deep joy in creating liturgy, as well as her skill in confronting hard questions. For Peter, David, and some of the other men with background in government service, duty was not a negative word or a joyless prospect, but the conversation began to polarize between men and women.

In a strong email to the SNDG, Brenda communicated her thoughts about the issues of power, leadership, and authority, which she saw in the discussion about what to call the staff team:

> I am sensing some confusion over how we describe power within the community. I agree with everyone that the locus of authority to make decisions for the community lies in Stewards, but I do not think that we can call that leadership, or if it is, then it is a different kind of leadership than what we are naming for the staff. . . . I think Stewards also has another kind of authority; it is collectively the place where God's call for the community is voiced and heard

and in some measure discerned. It is the visioning body of the community.

I think that what the Servant Leadership team provides us with is the leadership that is necessary to help Stewards make the decisions it needs to make, i.e. by creating Steward's agendas, and holding it to the commitments it has made, its articulated vision, its stated goals, and the new leadings of the Spirit that are discerned.... Stewards has ENTRUSTED this group with this power and authority.

Brenda's email shifted the conversation. Instead of referring to staffing needs, she used the term "Servant Leadership team" to describe their role for Stewards. She clearly did not regard them as administrative staff, and she did not repeat the "hot button" by calling them the "leadership team."

Not long afterwards, Brenda sent an email to the SDNG stating her call to "the Servant Leadership Team." As the child of missionary parents, Brenda had grown up in Japan. Now she ran her own business as a lawyer, specializing in Japanese patent disputes. Brenda's time availability would have seasons of demand away from home, but because her interests lay with hospitality and the relational life of the community, her call seemed to complement Jeanne's interest in public affairs. Soon Brenda's call was confirmed by the Stewards.

By then, we were referring to the staff as our "servant leadership team," taking the name from Brenda's email and Robert Greenleaf's essay "The Servant as Leader." In his essay, Greenleaf described a servant as one who lives and works "in service to a larger goal."[3] He identified a leader as one who can "see things whole," along with focusing on a particular part. That seemed to describe the leadership needs at Seekers perfectly, and the term *servant leadership* began to permeate our conversations.

To put all members of the new Servant Leadership Team (SLT) on an even footing, Kate dropped her time commitment back to one day a week. Peter had been paid for one day a week all along, and in November, Brenda and Jeanne were added at one day a week, making the SLT (as Peter joked) "Three lady lawyers and an old airborne ranger." It was a wry comment on their work experience outside of Seekers, and it downplayed the spiritual leadership, community trust, and different gifts that each one brought, but it gave them a certain humorous identity as they began to work together.

---

3. Greenleaf, *Servant Leadership*, 45.

Stalking the Spirit

Forming the SLT after Sonya's departure solidified the transition from the organizational period, led by a ministry team around Sonya, to a more organic and relational period of widely distributed leadership at Seekers. How the new servant leadership team would function as we moved from 2025 to Carroll Street would shape the next chapters of Seekers' story.

12

Manna in the Desert
Disciplined by Waiting

WITH THE BUILDING LOOMING in the distance like a ghost, anxiety over when and how Seekers would make the transition was being played out in many ways. Our structures worked against granting authority to anyone, even at the point of their gifts, although we had no trouble granting that authority to a mission group. How to handle disagreements between Stewards without hijacking the time and attention of everyone continued to plague us. Experience in pastoral care bumped against preconceptions about the authority and responsibilities of the Servant Leadership Team and of Stewards. We had much to learn in order to operate more relationally, as an organic body with distributed leadership.

As we waited, expecting to be in the new building by Easter 2003, Keith Seat led the Stewards in a brainstorming session about ways to introduce Seekers to the Takoma Park community. Creative ideas poured forth, but only the website garnered volunteers. Would the Servant Leadership Team (SLT) take care of the rest?

Guidelines for use of the space at Carroll Street by Seekers and "outside users" were drawn up by Jeanne, who took on that role for the SLT. Jeanne lived near the new building, was familiar with the community, and wanted to expand Seekers' outreach there. When she presented the guidelines, other Stewards began imagining all sorts of scenarios, special cases and complications. Micromanaging appeared to be one way of dealing with our anxiety. The note-taker commented: "The guidelines were approved after her plea to trust the SLT with evolution & application."

Jeanne was clear about wanting to spend more of her time pastoring and envisioning a more streamlined structure for Stewards, but we were reluctant to affirm those gifts, no matter how much they were needed. She wanted to work two days a week, but Stewards stubbornly held to equal time among the SLT members. Peter and Brenda were still working elsewhere, and Kate had just stepped back from two days a week in order to put everyone on the SLT on an equal footing. We were loathe to give Jeanne more authority, and seemed unable to address the issue openly.

OVERSEAS CONNECTIONS

In the wings, Roy Barber continued to build a connection between Seekers and the Bokamoso Youth Center in Winterveldt, South Africa. He arranged a yearly exchange between his students at St. Andrews Episcopal School in Potomoc, Maryland, and a selected group of twelve students from Bokamoso, who would come to the U.S. for a month of fundraising appearances and educational opportunities. Because they needed a non-profit sponsor, Seekers became the official host, although the parents of St. Andrews students actually housed the visitors.

The Bokamoso youth also spent a week at George Washington University, hosted by the drama department there. Seekers started a workshop for coaching the South African students with job skills, site visits, and resume presentation during each visit, to help them get jobs back in South Africa. In the subsequent decade, that vocational workshop has given many Seekers a three-day intensive experience with each visiting Bokamoso group.

About the same time, Seekers began to support a yearly work pilgrimage to Guatemala. When I retired as executive director of Faith@Work in 2002, Peter and I volunteered to lead the first trip for F@W. Four Seekers joined twenty others from the national F@W network on that first pilgrimage, to help build a village school in the highlands of Chimaltenango. When the new director of F@W decided that the pilgrimage no longer fit with their mission, Seekers became the official sponsor. Even though people from beyond Seekers continue to be the majority of participants, there are usually four or five Seekers on each trip. In many ways, the yearly work pilgrimage has become, for Seekers, the summer counterpart of the winter Bokamoso visit.

ANTICIPATION

2003 brought a reshuffling of Stewards into new mission groups as we anticipated the move to Carroll Street. Other working groups were busy with particular tasks, though they lacked the internal accountability structures of a mission group. SLT recognized the need to declare these groups as representatives of Seekers, so they asked Stewards to bless some of those ministry teams officially. That was done during worship, so the whole community would know about them, and feel free to join a task group if it felt like call. The need to share the workload more widely pushed us toward improvisation as we experimented with more distributed forms of leadership.

The creative artists in our midst kept hope alive during the cold, wet winter months of 2003. A sample of the bentwood chairs arrived from the designer, Peter Danko, and we began to imagine sitting in them for worship. Others made the trip out to Burkittsville, Maryland, to see the cross and altar table that had been handmade by John Schultz, who had been encouraged so long ago by a Growing Edge grant for his first wood lathe. They reported it was "simply beautiful—like the ones we are used to in the sanctuary of 2025 and yet different."

A new member, Bill Wilson, began work on a movable curved wall on which the cross would hang as a backdrop for our worship space. Peter assisted Kathryn Wysockey-Johnson, a young sculptor who was studying at the Corcoran Institute, to design a large round mosaic for the front of the church. It would be based on the design of our Communion set. Glen helped them to engineer a frame that could be secured to the outside of the building. Deborah and Peter also began to work with parts of the mosaic design as a "family" of covers for different publications, including a new brochure and the website, planning to make it as inviting as the building would be. Although we were feeling a bit like Israelites in the desert, waiting and watching for the PROMISED LAND, it was also apparent that long months of incubating our call to this new location were finally bearing fruit. The space began to fill with our dreams even though construction was painfully slow.

At the urging of more relational Stewards who were not meeting with the spirit guides, core members again turned their attention to the quality and content of their meetings. Jeanne asked everyone to write a paper on "the meaning of Stewards," and when she summarized the results she reported that there was general agreement that the primary function of Stewards is "holding or caring for the welfare of the whole," but there was real disagreement as to what constituted "spiritual grounding." Some saw our work as "building the body of Christ," and others saw it "primarily as administrative work," she said. Answers seemed to reflect an old division among Stewards. Was it primarily a place of belonging or decision-making? Spiritual formation or administration?

To release some Stewards from the tasks of decision-making, Jeanne suggested that Stewards have a council for handling the administrative work that needed to be done. It was a different version of separating Mary from Martha Stewards, and although the possibility of having a council generated some interest, the debate moved into old tracks. Some Stewards, who had no real sense of belonging or spiritual formation in their mission groups, felt the need for more personal sharing in our monthly meetings. Others felt their spiritual needs for accountability and confession were being met in weekly mission group structures, so they came to Stewards more ready for work. As the oldest members of Stewards and one of our founding members, Emily reminded us that we are "doing theology" in these policy discussions, and not simply making decisions. Once again, the council proposal didn't garner enough support to be implemented.

During this time, the Building Development Team was meeting at Carroll Street every Friday at 7:30 a.m., to oversee the renovation and make on-site decisions with the contractor. Others joined them for particular phases of the project, but for more than two years Keith, Peter, Deborah, and Glen "held the building" for us as other parts of the body of Seekers struggled to remain hopeful and committed.

WELLSPRING TURNS FIFTY

The fiftieth anniversary of Wellspring, the conference center at Dayspring Farm, brought a large crowd of past and present members of the wider Church of the Saviour community out to Dayspring on June 1, 2003. It was a gorgeous day, and people seemed glad to celebrate the story of how the Wellspring mission group had exposed so many people from across the country to the inward/outward focus of Church of the Saviour. Gordon and Mary Cosby were honored, and early members were featured in a short play.

As the afternoon presentations drew to a close, the heavens opened and rain poured down in torrents. Everyone ran to the Wellspring center, where a catered meal was waiting. There, Gordon urged the second-generation churches "to begin telling their story to the world." He gave his blessing to the differences that had developed among the second-generation churches, and spoke of his own dreams as well. Never interested in retirement, Gordon was being energized by starting "spiritual support groups" for post-incarceration men and women, which he called "Becoming Church."

Gordon's invitation to "tell our story" was welcomed by Seekers. Stewards had authorized me to create this history of Seekers, and several different Seekers had already produced a number of written resources based on our experience as a lay-led church. The discipline of weekly written reports has promoted writing and reflection, the "open pulpit" and posting sermons on the web has encouraged many people toward serious theological reflection, and our commitment to shared leadership has encouraged multiple voices to speak from our experience of call and ministry in daily life.[1]

---

1. Appendix 8.

C OF S CONSTITUTION REVISED

As a reminder that other communities of C of S were having their own troubles, we got word that the Church of the Servant Jesus had decided to disband. Coupled with the loss of income that would result when Seekers moved to Carroll Street, we wondered about the future of the ecumenical service at 2025. Gordon would be eighty-seven in July, and though his health was good and his call to preach was still strong, ending the Church of the Servant Jesus seemed to be a harbinger of other changes.

It had been ten years since Gordon invited dissolution of C of S and separate incorporation of the offspring churches. We learned from Kate Cudlipp, chair of the C of S council, that Gordon was in conversation about the possible sale of 2025, so we took a quick count of members to see who would be able to vote on such a sale. In 1993, just prior to the vote that led to separate incorporation, there had been twenty-one Seekers (out of a total of 125 C of S members) who were qualified to vote. According to our records, there were now just twelve Stewards who were dual members and could therefore vote on the sale of the building. We knew the other churches had experienced similar attrition, and wondered how many dual members were still active.

Although the sale of 2025 did not go through that year, Kate and Keith brought their legal skills to revamping the governance documents for the wider church. By 2006, when the vote to change the C of S bylaws was actually taken, the total number of dual members was down to fifty-four, and there were only eleven Seekers qualified to vote on the new constitution, so the shift to member churches was timely. From then on, dual membership was eliminated and any core member of a C of S council church could vote on matters of common purpose.

A DAY TO LEAP?

Our move seemed imminent as 2004 dawned, so a transition service at 2025 was planned for the Leap Year Sunday, February 29. David Lloyd was selected to preach at both Seekers and the ecumenical service, and we planned special food for a party after the second service. Stewards chose to make a gift of Deborah's copper hanging, which had been made to surround the cross at 2025, to the ecumenical service. The decorating team marked all the furniture and other belongings. But we could not move without clearance from the District government, and so we waited once again.

Energy for the inward journey seemed low as we anticipated the move, and the spirit guides decided to end their journey together. After meeting every month for three years, the spirit guides gave an overview of their work to Stewards. To develop skills for pastoral care, they had studied *Holy Listening* by Margaret Guenther and *The Art of Spiritual Guidance* by Carolyn Gratton, practiced group spiritual direction on each other, worked with the Enneagram, practiced techniques for deep listening and "clearness committee" discernment, taken time to name and bless gifts in each other, and practiced responding to written reports. As one of the independent groups for peer development, the spirit guides had certainly been faithful to their intentions for strengthening our community pastoring capabilities.

For the spring overnight at Wellspring, Peter and Kathryn Wysockey-Johnson brought the mosaic that we would eventually hang on the front of the building. Everyone was invited to bring pottery to be broken and added to the mosaic. The design was a simplified and colorful version of the design on our Communion set, and the motif has since become our publishing logo. It was a simple project, but it gave everyone a chance to participate directly.

Since nobody had stepped forward to manage the building on Carroll Street, the SLT held it for us. Stewards agreed that we might trade office space for daytime presence (using the model of Elizabeth O'Connor at 2025), and that we should consider whether an overall "building manager" should be part of the SLT. Jeanne agreed to continue as the primary contact on SLT for building use, but not for building care. How that would be accomplished was anybody's guess.

The long years between the vote to disband in 1994 and our move in 2004 took a toll on our spirits and toughened us up as well. Worship continued to be vital and lively. Our children grew up and left. New mission groups were born and others died. Giving continued to be strong and we had enough money in the bank to complete the renovation. Sonya moved and the new Servant Leadership Team offered steady guidance in the midst of a strong group of Stewards. As we stood on the brink of a new land for Seekers, everyone was more than ready to move, whether or not they liked the new location.

13

Home at Last!
Settling in at Carroll Street

ON JUNE 20, 2004, Seekers marched from our old home at 2025 Massachusetts Avenue to our new home at 276 Carroll Street NW, carrying the starburst banner made by Margreta Silverstone and the etched copper cross made by Deborah Sokolove. About thirty Seekers made the five-mile trek up through the District of Columbia to its northern border on Carroll Street.

When we arrived at the newly renovated building, Celebration Circle offered a liturgy of blessing in thanks to God for keeping us together as a community. Using an evergreen branch, Deborah and Peter sprinkled the portals with salty water and blessed the handmade altar, cross, and lectern, the curved reredos wall, and the chairs so carefully chosen for comfort and design. We sang Brian Wren's hymn of gladness, "This Is the Day of New Beginnings," with all of the hopes we had carried for the past ten years, then settled the banners into wooden stands made by David Lloyd. Using a liturgy that Kate Amoss shaped, the congregation moved through the building from room to room, chanting and singing favorite hymns, blessing the handmade crosses that had been mounted behind plexiglass at the eye level of a small child in each room. When the service was ended, there was a sense that we had truly arrived in the place God had promised. Finally, the work of making it our home could begin.

CHURCH GATHERED

Sunday morning worship continued to be the heartbeat of Seekers as a gathered community. Circle time marked the beginning of worship at the street level, to hear announcements, share news, and sing to those with a birthday that week. The peace and justice candle was introduced as a way to prayerfully name a justice issue held by someone in the community, who would then lead us in silence from the downstairs gathering time to the sanctuary upstairs. There, the quiet beauty of the room under a slightly raised dome in the center set the mood for worship.

Celebration Circle (CC) experimented with sound, light, and arranging the space for worship. The altar table moved from the corner to the center of the room and back again, depending on the liturgical season and theme. Chairs made the space adaptable for different configurations. We made space for dance or drama when that was part of the liturgy. We learned that the raised dome in the center of the sanctuary worked with the wooden floor to make the room as resonant and lively as we had hoped, perfect for congregational singing and musical performances. CC used the vertical space to weave ribbons, hang a canopy, and manage lighting in different ways. During Advent, it took a while for people to notice the projected star that was moving toward the altar. Each season brought some new burst of creativity from CC as they designed a new liturgy, created new bulletins, and experimented with the space.

In the first year, CC made sure that we heard many different voices from the open pulpit, and we reveled in the expansiveness of time without having to make room for the second service. Worship often stretched to ninety minutes or more. Afterwards, people gathered in the large friendly kitchen area for coffee, and we began scheduling special meetings in the skylight room after worship. Those open forums included budget discussions, a chance to go deeper with a guest preacher, and sometimes an introduction to Seekers for newcomers. Now they take place every third Sunday so people can plan to stay late after worship on that day.

NEIGHBORHOOD OUTREACH

Posters for the first art day camp were put up immediately after we arrived, in order to attract neighborhood children. Martha Phillips had been confident of the need, and the Artists' Group was ready to support her. We learned that the Artists' Group would have to get criminal background checks with the DC government in order to work with these children, and so they did that. Soon the roster was full, and the week-long camp confirmed that the downstairs space had been well planned for such use.

The Servant Leadership Team announced plans for a neighborhood open house to invite groups that might be interested in renting our space for use during the week. Many people signed up to handle the Seekers display booth at the Takoma Park Folk Festival, where Jesse Palidofsky would be one of the musical hosts. Some saw the festival as a place where children might be attracted to Seekers, so children were included in staffing the booth. Others linked Seekers to the local Fourth of July parade as a way to reach out to the community.

Then the Building Development Team brought a financial dilemma to Stewards. Work on the building had cost Manna significantly more than the contract called for, and Keith wanted some guidance about how to handle the extra costs, which had been rounded down to $85,000. After much discussion, we decided to make a $40,000 payment from our operating budget for the work that had been completed, and then, in six months, we would make a $45,000 gift in gratitude for Manna's stretch to finish the job. Since we had been supporting Manna as a housing rehabilitation ministry for many years, there was some grumbling about how the cost overrun might have happened, but we were so glad to be in the new building that anything seemed reasonable.

Another Seeker tended the garden and grounds in back of the church. A rambling yellow rose, which someone had saved from the rubble of the building and replanted by the back porch, bloomed profusely as spring came round again, like a biblical "root out of dry ground." That year, the men came back from their spring retreat at Rolling Ridge singing "The Rose" in fabulous harmony, and it has become a standard to close the monthly sing-alongs.

COMMITMENT AND INCLUSION

A short-lived mission group, Seeds of Hope, focused on republishing our basic pamphlets and reaching out to other churches that might be interested in learning about our structures for empowering ministry in daily life. Although the group made several presentations, there was no long-term call to keep it together, so the group disbanded. As part of their effort however,

Peter created a colorful "organizational chart" that looked like a starburst of mission groups gathered around our central experience of worship, and turned it into a PowerPoint presentation to give others a visual summary of Seekers. He identified Seekers as a community of faith "at the crossroads of commitment and inclusion," with structures that invite many people to participate in worship, practice accountability and mission together, and take ministry in daily life seriously. Now that our website is attracting visitors and seminary students who are interested in different models for "being church," the pamphlets and PowerPoint presentation have helped us understand who we are and how we actually function. The questions for emerging churches, listed in the appendix, gradually developed as different groups inquired about the practices that hold this particular body of Christ together.[1] The effort that began so long ago, to find an image that would describe Seekers on the letterhead of our stationary, has finally found a form that feels right—at least for now.

Although Seekers began to attract people from the neighborhood through the twelve-step meetings and community groups that met in our building, we wanted to retain the practice of encouraging commitment for anyone who wanted to become a member. Inclusion carried an element of intentionality. Since Stewards had decided to open membership to anybody who wanted to be intentional about developing their spiritual lives, the process of moving into general membership was updated. In addition to regular worship with Seekers, we expected potential members to attend a class in the School of Christian Living, request a shepherding relationship with a Steward, and contribute regularly. We wanted to move people beyond an individualistic understanding of faith, toward becoming part of a *body of Christ*.

Commitment to following Jesus is an expectation for all Stewards. We affirmed the expectation that all Stewards would belong to a mission group, and that every mission group would have at least two Stewards in it, to link each group with the decision-making body of Stewards. Then, as though to reassure each other that the Stewards could be depended upon as healthy ligaments of Christ's body at Carroll Street, all of the eighteen Stewards chose to recommit in October of 2004.

While this restatement of our values and structures was taking place, Peter created a humorous booklet titled "Who's in Charge Around Here" to identify groups and leaders for various aspects of our life together. Our

1. Appendix 9.

practice of distributed leadership was confusing to people who were used to a more hierarchical structure, and the booklet helped each group identify the parts of our common life that they were responsible for.

ENDINGS

Our new home was no guarantee of permanence or stability. In the fall of 2004, Linda Strand died suddenly of an aneurism at age fifty-seven. Her death tested our capacity for pastoral care by a mission group, and we found it resilient and sturdy. Because they lived in Virginia, Linda's husband, Mike, called Peter as their "pastor," and her mission group, for immediate support. From the mission group, Cynthia Dahlin helped Mike navigate the hospital regulations as the family chose to remove life support. I made an unfired urn to hold Linda's ashes, and Peter led a family memorial service out at Dayspring, which culminated with Mike and their three daughters scattering Linda's ashes in the Lake of the Saints. Later, Mike installed a bench near the labyrinth at Dayspring to honor Linda, making it a special place of remembrance for Seekers on silent retreat. It was another expression of belonging to the land at Dayspring as an extension of our life together.

Emily Gilbert continued to press Stewards to meet in Virginia periodically in order to ease the travel time for herself and other older members who lived there. But rather than changing the venue for Stewards, Jeanne helped Emily decide to ask for status as an "emerita Steward," with the option of coming to any meetings that she was especially interested in. Emily wanted to continue coming to worship, meeting with her mission group, supporting Seekers financially, and participating in special events, but she wasn't able to make two long driving trips on the first Sunday of each month in order to attend Stewards. We were glad to grant Emily that status, making her our first emerita Steward. Muriel Lipp, who also lived in Virginia, has since joined Emily as an emerita Steward. They were the last Stewards to have been members of the parent church. All of the remaining Stewards have been shaped by the culture of shared leadership at Seekers.

In spite of our efforts to attract new families with children, newcomers at our new location were mainly middle-aged people who found us on the website. Some expressed a desire to "go deeper" now that their families were launched, and others were drawn by the sense of community at Seekers. In order to receive these newcomers, and support them until they found their way to classes in the School, Brenda decided to leave her mission group,

Journeying with Children, to call a new mission group for hospitality. In spite of our expressed willingness to let groups die if there was no called leadership, ending a long-lasting mission group like Journeying with Children felt like failure. After all the effort to find a home with play space for children, there were now too few children to "journey with." It was time for the mission group to end.

Jeanne Marcus then announced that she would be setting down her responsibility for the scheduling use of the building. She agreed to write a job description for the building use coordinator, since she was now familiar with the tasks involved: keeping the calendar, meeting with prospective renters to show them the space and go over the security system, collecting monies owed to Seekers, and avoiding scheduling conflicts. FOG thought we could offer somebody a stipend to oversee use of the building, since we wanted maximum use of the space by Seekers and others too. Money for that purpose was put in the 2005 budget, but Jeanne was clear that she did not consider it her call and would not apply for the job.

BEGINNINGS

Along with endings, there were also new beginnings in the fresh, spare space at Carroll Street. The call of the Koinonia mission group, to welcome newcomers and coordinate celebrations, was confirmed by Stewards. Koinonia planned a celebratory breakfast before the service on Easter morning, and they anticipated weddings, anniversaries, and birthday parties. They soon outfitted the kitchen with Guatemalan placemats and cloth napkins for use by the School, along with festive linens for Easter and Christmas. The building and its seating flexibility encouraged experimentation and celebration, and Koinonia was a new wineskin for the new life that was beginning to bubble up at Seekers.

Peter picked up Jeanne's responsibility for the building while the SLT continued to seek the right person for that job. By then, Peter had retired from Communities in Schools and was more able to offer the attention needed, even though the travel distance from Virginia was a hindrance for him. That year, Washington Storytellers rented the downstairs office, and Liz Lerman's dance troupe used the open sanctuary space while their space was being renovated. The Time & Space (T&S) mission group then formed as seven people committed themselves to care for the building. Peter and Deborah joined as an extension of their work with the Building

Home at Last!

Development Team, even though it meant belonging to both Celebration Circle and T&S.

Another new wineskin meant a significant loss for Seekers. In July 2005, Jeanne expressed her doubts about continuing on the SLT, and by September she was clear about leaving the leadership team at Seekers. She was taking more training in nonviolent communication, and named the burden of managing the building during the preceding year as part of her decision. She left the leadership team with a ritual of thanks during worship, and did not recommit as a Steward. For Seekers, Jeanne had brought gifts, vision, and call at the very time we were struggling the most over losing Sonya and waiting for the renovation of Carroll Street to be completed. Everyone was truly grateful for Jeanne's leadership during the transition. Once again, the timing seemed providential.

Stewards decided not to seek another member for the SLT right away, but to watch how mission groups might pick up more of the pastoral care for their members. T&S then created a job description and made a detailed list of tasks for a new building use coordinator. Not long after the job description was circulated, T&S hired Katie Fisher, a new member of Seekers, to be the building manager. Although Katie lives far away, she interacts with prospective users of the building, is accountable to T&S, and is keeping the building actively in use. Once again, the ability to wait for the Spirit's provision seemed to bring the right person at just the right time.

Learners & Teachers exercised their authority at the point of call when they proposed shorter classes for the School of Christian Living, in the interest of attracting more people who could commit to six weeks instead of ten or twelve. By shortening the classes, L&T sacrificed a certain depth of community on the altar of pragmatism. They knew that mission groups would have to do more of the spiritual formation that the School had provided before, but it was easier to recruit teachers and find students for a shorter term, so L&T settled into a rhythm of offering two classes at a time, usually one biblical class and one spiritual growth class.

InterPlay, a particular form of expressive movement, also took root in the new space at Seekers. Before we were at Carroll Street, Sue Johnson had convinced Stewards to sponsor a weekend with InterPlay's founders from California. When the building wasn't finished in time, that weekend had to be held at the Takoma Park Presbyterian Church. By the time we did move into the building, Kate and Billy Amoss had begun their leadership training with InterPlay, and soon there were monthly "open sessions" in the sanctuary as well as more intensive Saturday sessions for prospective leaders. The open sessions were designed to attract newcomers and to provide practice for those in the leadership training program. During Advent, Billy and Kate offered Interplay "forms" to the readings on each successive Sunday. Many of the men in Seekers attended a men's InterPlay event at Wellspring, and since then several other Seekers have completed the leadership training program. InterPlay seems like a natural form of embodied spirituality for Seekers.

To round out 2005, the Silverstones returned from Guatemala on Christmas Eve with their newly adopted son, Oslin. Both parents had participated in the annual Guatemala pilgrimage, had decided afterward to apply for an international adoption, and had been through the grueling adoption process. Just a year old, Oslin was introduced at the gala Christmas Eve potluck in the sanctuary, and soon was wrapped in a quilt made with squares that had been created by many different Seekers. Oslin's arrival was a sign of new life for Seekers, embodying our love for children and our embrace of the wider world. Since Margreta is a nationally known quilter, making a quilt for Oslin was also a heartfelt gift from all of us.

UNDERCURRENTS

Along with signs of new life in our new place, there were undercurrents of dissatisfaction in the community. Talk about Stewards needing to be more spiritual, more relational, and more skillful about dealing with conflict surfaced once again. Was it a longing for more leadership? Nostalgia for Sonya? Relief after the tension of waiting? A desire to participate in decisions without the commitment to carry them through? Envy of those in visible positions? Unmet needs and feelings of disappointment swirled around in our new space.

In response to those undercurrents, the SLT (Peter, Kate, and Brenda) decided to make the spring overnight a gathering to address some of these complaints, so they hired an outside consultant to guide the process. A questionnaire was sent to everyone in the congregation. Thirty-five people gave written responses and forty people came to the overnight. The group identified these familiar unmet needs:

1. pastoring Seekers who were not in mission groups;

2. community-wide involvement in decision-making;

Home at Last!

3. developing better listening practices for conflict resolution;

4. questions about whether the structures (i.e., Stewards, mission groups, and work teams) could carry our vision.

At the overnight, Celebration Circle felt particularly targeted for criticism. People complained that the worship was not as creative or inspiring as it had been with Sonya, even though CC had been experimenting a lot with the new space. It also appeared that some people were expecting more pastoral care from our visible worship leaders (the liturgists from CC) than they could provide as equal partners in creating our life together. Without Sonya to smooth things over, we were being asked to grow up and work with each other as peers. Some were not ready.

To address some of the issues, there was a congregational meeting after worship. We divided into four discussion groups around those four topics, to listen and learn from each other, but that did not assuage much of the dissatisfaction. For awhile, the primary dissenters met with Kate in an effort to find a way together. In the end, however, two of them simply left. The others stayed and have become part of our pattern of more widely distributed leadership.

After all these complaints, Stewards were relieved to find that our contributed income was still flowing outward with a sense of generosity and commitment to healing the world. In the 2006 budget, giving to missions amounted to 29 percent of our total budget, and we promised ourselves to move that percentage upward toward 40 percent as soon as we figured out what the building costs would be. Stewards also decided to consider building income and expense as a separate item, designated "ministry of place." We were glad to see that debt service and building operations (less building income) came to 28 percent of the budget, up some from the 20 percent we had allocated for space in our first year of existence. For those who feared that owning a building would soak up all of our financial resources, it was good news indeed, even though we still had a sizable debt to pay off. We agreed to pay off the debt, which was owed mainly to members of Seekers, at a rate of $50,000 a year, which would allow us to complete repayment in ten years. We thought we could handle that out of our operating expenses.

Over thirty years, the Seekers' budget had increased tenfold, from $25,000 to $250,000, although the number of people was about the same. Stewards were still contributing about 75 percent of the annual income because of their commitment to tithing. Those figures gave Stewards a sense that we were headed in the right direction, in spite of the complaints that we weren't being relational and inclusive enough.

14

Practicing Ministry in Daily Life
Seekers Gathered and Sent

AFTER TEN YEARS IN our new location, Seekers has become more open and diverse as a worshiping body, while the committed core of Stewards and mission groups gives it strength and resilience. We are now a Christian community of approximately fifty adults and ten children, still in search of God's guidance for living out call in the daily structures of our lives.

We are also an aging congregation with fewer children than before, but we continue to attract newcomers who are bringing different needs for understanding call in the second half of life. Because of our location, on the street, near a Metro stop and across from a 7-Eleven store, we are also attracting more homeless or precariously situated people. For all of us, belonging to Seekers brings support, encouragement, and challenges to grow in spirit and in truth.

Our weekly worship continues to be vital and creative. The open pulpit brings a different voice to interpret the lectionary scriptures each week. Our tradition of shared leadership means that many functions that are usually carried by clergy (preaching, teaching, pastoral care, administration, etc.) are carried by Stewards, the Servant Leadership Team, mission groups, or individuals recognized for particular gifts or experiences. Over time we have examined our structures, nurtured our relationships with God and each other, settled into our new home, and discovered new missions (external) and ministries (internal) as a result of our new location.

JOURNEY OUTWARD

When we disperse to live out "Christian servanthood in the structures of daily life," as our call says, we are a very scattered community, like yeast in the organizations and institutions of our culture. Many Seekers are involved in some form of advocacy for vulnerable populations, particularly children and elders. Even those who have retired from full-time work are involved in many different forms of part-time paid or volunteer work as followers of Jesus. We depend on Seekers for inspiration and accountability, for encouragement and challenge to grow and serve.

The Seekers website quickly became an important way of inviting newcomers toward Seekers. When two younger women came to Seekers through the C of S Discipleship Year, they brought new energy and expertise in web-based graphic design, and that led to another ad hoc group to make the website more attractive and interactive. Jeffrey was honored for his work as the volunteer webmaster and, in addition to the volunteer group from Seekers, we hired a design team to build a new website to expand our presence in the world: www.seekerschurch.org.

Over time, the Seekers Web Information Management Team (SWIM) formalized its structure and process, but did not become a mission group, since most people were already in another place of spiritual accountability. The SWIM team established format guidelines and editorial responsibilities, and created links with earlier sermons and liturgies. Although they experimented with giving mission groups direct access to updating sections of the website, we discovered (again) that one group needs to have specific responsibility for a piece of our ministry. The SWIM team has since become part of the Time & Space mission group, and they keep the website current.

The building at 276 Carroll Street has truly become a Ministry of Place, tended by the Time & Space mission group. It is being well used during the week, and we know ourselves to be "a Christian community with an *interfaith* welcome." Katie has proven to be a good space coordinator, pairing congenial groups for use of the downstairs conference room and the upstairs sanctuary, and coaching the many different users to be respectful of each other. In addition to the Covenant Community, a small church of mostly African-American women, there is a Science of Spirituality meditation group, Buddhist offerings of vegetarian cooking from our kitchen, and the Fabringen Community rents the whole building to celebrate their Jewish Holy Days.

Practicing Ministry in Daily Life

Art and *advocacy*, the charisms of Seekers, dance together at Carroll Street, as InterPlay, YogaRhythmics, summer music camp, Argentine tango, and local theater productions have also put down roots for regular practice in our building. The T&S mission group sponsors a quarterly gathering for regular users of the building in an effort to create another level of community beyond Seekers—another way for us to "welcome the stranger." In her year-end report to Stewards, Katie described an astounding total of 656 events by forty different organizations *other than* Seekers during 2011. Of those, ten were interfaith religious groups, and the rest were mostly non-profit and civic groups.

Owning a building has given birth to other missions for Seekers. Out of conversations and a film series on race and diversity, another mission group formed. Known as the Eyes to See, Ears to Hear, Peace Prayer mission group (Is2C), members had been meeting for several years to pray about social justice issues. The group sponsored a summer peace camp for children and invited Seekers to participate in "sacred conversations" on race and diversity with the Covenant Community. Is2C has taken the lead on political issues, like the anti-torture campaign, and urged Seekers to participate with Covenant Community in their annual Thanksgiving grocery box distribution. More recently, Is2C has been involved with a wider C of S conversation on racial reconciliation and incarceration patterns in America, inviting other Seekers to be more involved.

Another outward mission is the Carroll Café, a monthly venue for local folk music artists. Jesse Palidofsky and Glen Yakushiji had dreamed of such an outlet during the long renovation process, and Glen made sure that we had a high-quality sound and light system to support public performances. As a performing artist himself, Jesse uses his contacts for programming professional recording artists for the monthly concerts, and he is also using the church as a place to practice and compose music as well. Although he continues to work as a part-time hospice chaplain, Jesse has released one album of his music and is working on a second. While none of these missions were undertaken for the purpose of drawing new members to Seekers, all have been points of contact for people who are interested in outward service for the common good.

A different aspect of Seekers' outward journey is our relationship with the other C of S churches. Because we still own the Dayspring property together, that connection is still important. Kate Cudlipp kept us connected with other missions in the wider C of S community as she continued to chair the C of S council along with her SLT responsibilities. Although our location has made it difficult to participate in missions along Columbia Road, many Seekers have individual ties with C of S non-profits (Manna, Jubilee Jobs, The Potter's House, and Joseph's House), which also guides our giving to those ministries.

As described earlier, Kate and Keith Seat, the Seekers representative to the C of S council, reworked the C of S bylaws in 2006 to allow core members of any church represented on the council to vote on disposition of 2025 or Dayspring. Two years after the new constitution was adopted, the headquarters building of Church of the Saviour, at 2025 Massachusetts Avenue, was finally listed for sale. At ninety, Gordon Cosby had stopped preaching there, and the council affirmed Kayla McClurg as "the face of C of S." To maintain its identity as a church while 2025 was on the market, Kayla offered an informal worship service at 2025 until it was sold. She is the resident host at Andrews House, and continues as the "point person" for various C of S churches and separately incorporated missions from her office at the Festival Center. Kayla also nourishes the spiritual life of many through daily inspirational selections online, at InwardOutward.org.

COMMUNITY LIFE

There are now eight mission groups at Seekers, which provide a matrix of accountability for inner reflection and outer mission. These groups are still our primary way to belong and function with authority at Seekers. Four of the mission groups were started at 2025 (Celebration Circle, Learners & Teachers, Mission Support, and Living Water), and four new mission groups have been called into being at 276 Carroll Street: Koinonia, Time & Space, Eyes to See, and most recently Broken and Beloved, a group of healers who had been meeting informally for personal and professional support. With an average of five members each, those eight groups provide the backbone of accountability and pastoral care for about two-thirds of the congregation.

Mission groups not only provide a structure for collective outreach, they tend the inner life of Seekers as well. The "journey inward" still begins with personal disciplines of self-examination, mission group participation, and weekly worship at Seekers. Celebration Circle has continued to shape our understanding of Christ by writing liturgies that hold our lives at the crossroads of inclusion and commitment. In each new liturgical season, CC chooses a theme out of Scripture and community life, and creates a new liturgy for our worship together. Each one begins with a reflection paragraph that offers fresh poetic language and provocative images for contemplation before worship. Each liturgist from the mission group writes his or her own prayers with an eye toward the universal story, lectionary scriptures, current events, and life in Seekers. Because these liturgies are posted on our website, we now hear from small churches in distant places who also depend on Seekers for their liturgical inspiration. Some of those liturgies have been published by Abington Press in their three-volume lectionary series. More recently, Peter and Deborah have authored a book of lectionary-based prayers, *Calling on God*.[1]

The open pulpit at Seekers is certainly one of the unique features of our community. CC makes sure that everyone who preaches understands the responsibility of speaking some part of God's word for the community. Having a different preacher each week has not offered us the consistent visionary leadership that Gordon Cosby provided for C of S and Fred provided for Seekers in the first decade of our life together. However, the quality of preaching at Seekers is remarkably good, not only because we publish sermons on the Web for all to see, but because preachers take that responsibility seriously. For many years, we did not publish the names of scheduled preachers in order to avoid selective attendance, but now they can be found on the Seekers website for anyone who cares to look.

After worship, the Koinonia mission group sees to it that we have refreshments for coffee hour. The design of the building allows for everyone to fit into a country kitchen that feels homey and welcoming. Koinonia also makes sure that visitors are welcomed and, after several visits, added to the website, which we use to keep everyone informed of activities at the building. Koinonia also works closely with the Servant Leadership Team to track people who are not yet in a mission group, where they would receive pastoral care from the group.

On the third Sunday of each month, Learners & Teachers sponsors a meeting after worship to help newcomers understand our culture of commitment and generosity. It might be discussion of domestic or international giving, an introduction to the "semi-secrets of Seekers," a chance to hear more from one of our building's users, or simply a chance for everyone to discuss an issue of community interest. L&T also sponsors the School

---

1. Appendix 8.

of Christian Living on Tuesday nights. The Seekers SCL offers a regular menu of classes, which draw both newcomers and experienced members, and there is a real sense of communion in the table fellowship as we share a vegetarian meal together before classes begin. L&T tries to schedule classes that will build up the community, deepen our understanding of God's call, and equip us for mission and ministry. The six-week classes are also meant to give participants a taste of what it would be like to join a mission group, and classes are often a stepping-stone to deeper commitment.

Most other "regulars" are associated with task groups, where they may have a sense of community, but they do not write spiritual reports and often do not experience the challenge to grow that comes with real accountability. Although that is a point of concern for Stewards, we trust that the Spirit is at work and will show us the way forward. The question of how to offer spiritual companionship to those who would not or could not commit to a mission group continues to plague us, because the people who might be the logical spiritual guides are already committed to mission groups.

Silent retreats also continue to be an important discipline for tending one's inner journey at Seekers. The Living Water mission group has responsibility for silent retreats, and they have made an effort to reach out beyond Stewards for leadership of those retreats. By offering classes in journaling, prayer, and end-of-life issues at the school, LW has encouraged wider participation in our silent retreats at Dayspring. LW also sponsored a well-attended class on the Five Wishes, a popular instrument for describing end-of-life care. In addition, LW created a memorial wall in the back stairwell of our building, with natural slate and fused glass tiles, listing names with their birth and death dates. New tiles for any Seeker or immediate family member are added in time to be blessed on the Sunday closest to All Saints Day each year. Several Seekers have chosen to have their ashes scattered at Dayspring, so this gives us a way to keep our memory of them alive.

Seekers bought two shares (two full weeks) in Rolling Ridge, near Harpers Ferry in West Virginia, back when it was being formed on land used by the FLOC Wilderness School. Unlike Dayspring, with its open fields and single stream, Rolling Ridge offers rugged terrain and challenging hikes. Although we have not been regular about using those shares because of scheduling difficulties, the men of Seekers have had a yearly retreat at Rolling Ridge, and several mission groups go there for more of a wilderness experience. Two families also purchased shares in Stillpoint, a smaller residence at Rolling Ridge, and donated them to Seekers for community use.

Practicing Ministry in Daily Life

The Broken & Beloved mission group has taken responsibility for scheduling our use of those shares.

NEW CALLS

Community investment in cultivating new calls has continued through the Growing Edge Fund. Each year, small grants and one or two advocates accompany different members of Seekers as they test a possible call. One, the grant made to Roy Barber for travel to South Africa, has become a full-fledged foundation, based on the partnership between St. Andrews Episcopal School and the Bokamoso Youth Centre in Winterveld. Others, like a grant made to explore training as a hospital chaplain, have resulted in a clear "no" for the individual who thought he might want to do that. Being willing to support new calls in this way has become a mark of the Spirit at Seekers.

Beyond our commitment to ministry in daily life, the inward/outward journey for Seekers has been shaped by our new location, with large open windows facing onto the street. One result has been visibility and accessibility for people walking by. Two international refugees simply walked through the door, looking for sanctuary and a church home. One, a young woman from Rwanda, came seeking safety and asylum. Another, a former government official and torture victim from Uganda, arrived after he prayed for "the right church." Now Jackie and David have both obtained green cards, are working, and continue to enlarge our capacity for caring.

From Uganda, we have recently welcomed David's wife and six children—another chance for us to grow and change as a community. Along with several homeless men who have come to Seekers through twelve-step groups meeting in our building, we realized that our desire to be a more racially diverse congregation was simply happening naturally. We suddenly have a critical number to attract other people of color. Small teams have formed around each of these people to help provide financial and, more importantly, emotional and spiritual support. These informal teams have become crucibles for mutual learning beyond our mission group structures, and they will disband when no longer needed.

Another result of our presence on the street is a team of volunteers led by Jacob Folger, who was formerly homeless himself, to assemble a monthly supply of "care packs." These small drawstring backpacks include new socks, washcloths, personal care items like a toothbrush and toothpaste, and a granola bar or easy-to-open can of food. The bags also include information about local housing and food assistance, along with an invitation to attend Seekers. The team invited all Seekers to donate items for the care packs, and soon had enough to assemble about fifteen care packs every month. The team has encouraged anyone in Seekers to take a bag and give it to someone on the street in order to encourage personal contact. Stories of the project are posted on the Seeker's website, and the volunteers are developing a strong group identity. Although Seekers generally opts for systemic change, this kind of direct contact with real need has encouraged us to engage directly with people who come through the door because of our location next to a Metro stop, or who stop us on a street corner, asking for a handout.

Finally, as a natural result of our long-standing commitment to gender inclusiveness, the sanctuary fairly burst with joy at the wedding of Kate Cudlipp and her partner, Carole. After twenty-eight years together, they were already a committed couple. But when the District of Columbia finally made same-sex marriage legal in 2010, we were eager to celebrate their marriage. Peter and I were honored to officiate. Their wedding was both elegant and casual, as people gathered around tables that filled the upper floor for a candlelight dinner afterwards. For some of their gay and lesbian guests, it was surprising to be welcomed by a Christian church. For Seekers, it was a natural extension of our original call.

2025 Sold

On October 18, 2010, the stately brownstone on Massachusetts Avenue, which had served as the headquarters for Church of the Saviour for almost sixty years, was finally sold to the Zients family foundation. After funding the Faithful Servants Trust Fund and the C of S office for another year, each of the C of S churches received an equal share of the sale price. Dayspring Church got a double portion, in recognition of its challenging stewardship of our single remaining common property. About the same time, Gordon and Mary Cosby moved from their home in Virginia, near Mt. Vernon, to an apartment at Christ House, where they could get the nursing care that they needed and be closer to the other C of S missions on Columbia Road. Still active at ninety-two, Gordon continued to work at raising money for a credit union to serve poor people and participate in spiritual support groups until his death three years later.

Practicing Ministry in Daily Life

Seekers had been preparing for this windfall from the sale of 2025. We engaged the Faith and Money Network to help us think about how to invest that money for the common good. At Kate's invitation, others also came to speak at an open meeting after worship about social investing. Then Stewards decided to pay off the interest-bearing loans on our building, continue our investment with Manna for housing rehabilitation, invest funds in City First Bank, a local bank lending to projects on the East (poorer) side of Washington, DC, and put the remaining money in OikoCredit for international microcredit lending. That decision followed our guidelines for advocacy and bequests—to invest in organizations committed to social justice. Our legacy from 2025 will supply banking services for underserved populations, and still be available for a new mission if needed.

Once the sale of 2025 had been completed, attention turned to the Dayspring property, which the C of S churches still own together. In November of 2010, the Wellspring Mission Group set down its call to manage the conference center, and Dayspring Church was charged by the council to lead a discernment process about its use. Although located on Dayspring property, Wellspring had functioned as a C of S mission group since its inception, and now that Gordon was no longer casting a vision for Church of the Saviour, the question of purpose for Wellspring had to be faced.

It was not easy to convince the related C of S churches to stretch their resources of time, talent, energy, and money to think about new uses for the five Wellspring buildings, because there was no automatic connection to its former mission (exposing people to the inward/outward journey of C of S). The discernment group, which included representatives from six of the nine C of S churches, met monthly for nearly a year to create a request for proposal. Of the proposals that came in, partnering with the Sandy Spring Friends School seemed to provide the right combination of stable income, common values, and potential for more cooperation in the area of environmental education. Dayspring Church then asked Keith to negotiate with Sandy Spring and help the wider C of S network imagine other uses for the whole Dayspring Farm. It seems Spirit-led that the organizational skills needed by some of our sister churches have been available from Seekers for this period of reimagining Church of the Saviour. Long-term stewardship of the Dayspring property is still an open question.

In many ways, owning a building has given Seekers a new sense of identity, and the freedom to join with other churches besides those birthed by C of S. Seekers took a step toward interfaith cooperation by joining

143

other churches to build a bargaining group for solar and wind power. The Is2C mission group sponsored a class on environmental awareness, and we are finding new connections with Dayspring's Earth Ministry as a result. Recognizing that there is a difference between being good stewards of the earth and listening to the earth and its creatures as God's voice, a number of Seekers are being drawn toward a new understanding of the treasure we hold in common at Dayspring.

ANOTHER ENDING

On July 23, 2011, Kate Cudlipp, a key member of our Servant Leadership Team, had a terrible bike accident. While riding alone in Rock Creek Park, she hit a pothole and pitched over the handlebars. Although she was wearing a helmet, her neck was broken. Bystanders gave her CPR and called 911. On a ventilator at Washington Hospital Center, she learned that she would never move, speak, eat, or breathe on her own again. Completely conscious and able to more her head slightly, she chose to have the ventilator removed in accordance with her Five Wishes directive. Kate died peacefully on July 28, with Carole and a small circle of friends at her side. As Carole said at the memorial service at Seekers, "Kate had been preparing for something new, something very different. We just never dreamed it would be this!"

Sobered by her sudden death, Seekers began to move on without Kate's steady hand. Our structures of shared leadership held steady, and let us grieve the many spaces where Kate had been. Brenda and Peter continued to offer themselves as the Servant Leadership Team while we identified the many things for Seekers and C of S that Kate had been doing. In worship and in Stewards, we felt most keenly the loss of Kate's strong voice for social justice.

In the wake of Kate's death, I was asked to be the new chair of the C of S council. When the Hubers set down their call to produce a C of S newspaper, the council authorized a smaller newsletter, *Callings*, which is designed to keep the C of S churches and independent ministries more connected. Although most of the C of S churches have websites of their own, our collective presence on the web consists of links from Kayla's website, InwardOutward.org. In each quarterly issue of *Callings* we feature one church and one C of S–related ministry, name the entire network of churches and separate ministries, and list upcoming events.

Another result of Kate's death was the need to pay off the last zero-percent loan for our building in order to close Kate's estate. It was a stretch, but we were able to do it without using our legacy from the sale of 2025, so now we own the building on Carroll Street free and clear.

Once the building was paid for, our budget designated 40 percent for external giving, our prebuilding level. And by the time we added earmarked giving ($70,000 in 2011), funding for external giving came to 50 percent of our contributed income. With a growing need for financial help among members of the congregation, we began looking at money as a common resource in new ways. That may mean more attention to microenterprise loans, as well as direct aid. It seems clear that giving remains an important spiritual discipline at Seekers.

NEW LEADERSHIP

After several months of mourning Kate's untimely death, and testing our resilience as a community, Brenda and Peter asked for a new discernment group to issue a call for one or two new members for the Servant Leadership Team. They identified Kate's *administrative skills* and her heart for *social justice* as major needs for the team.

A discernment group was formed with an equal number of members and Stewards. The discernment group was encouraged to revisit earlier documents that described our reasons for having some paid leadership at Seekers. Some also reread Robert Greenleaf's formative essay "The Servant as Leader," which had been the original source of our name, Seekers. Recently republished in book form, Greenleaf's SaLT essay described the dynamic of leadership and followership in this way: "[Followers] will freely respond only to individuals who are chosen as leaders because they are proven and trusted as servants."[2]

Although there were several Stewards who might have responded to the call, in the end only one person did. Trish Nemore, of the Eyes to See mission group, wrote a long letter describing what she perceived to be her call to the SLT. Although she said that she felt "unworthy" to fill Kate's shoes, she decided to write the letter of application as a way to test her call, because she would know at the end of the writing whether it was true. That balance of response to the Spirit and questioning the call itself seemed exactly right.

---

2. Greenleaf, *Servant Leadership*, 46.

Trish has had a distinguished career as a lawyer for Medicare advocacy, was a founding member of the Eyes to See mission group, and is known for her collaborative skills within Seekers. Set to retire within the year, she felt she would have time and energy for SLT. The discernment group recommended Trish without reservations. After meeting with anyone who gathered after worship to ask any questions they might have, Trish was confirmed by Stewards and installed as a member of the SLT (and presented with a ritual salt grinder) during worship on March 11, 2012.

While the SLT is not selected to represent different constituencies within Seekers, the three members of the SLT actually do that. Trish belongs to Eyes to See for outreach. Brenda belongs to Koinonia for community building, and Peter belongs to Celebration Circle for worship and Time & Space for building maintenance. Brenda and Trish both live in Maryland, where most of the newcomers to Seekers live. Peter lives in Virginia, where more of the older members live. Although they do not have formal theological training, all three members of the SLT have been keeping the disciplines of Stewards, and have been active participants in our School of Christian Living, both as learners and as teachers. Individually, they are gifted as servants, skilled as leaders, acquainted with grief, and capable in crisis situations. Together, they bring strong gifts for servant leadership among the fifteen active Stewards at Seekers.

Once again, we have weathered a major transition in leadership and continued to heed God's call to ministry in daily life. The congregation has changed from an exuberant collection of young families with children to one of more seasoned seekers and servant leaders. Our Ministry of Place has brought new people from the neighborhood into the church, and we have become a more diverse congregation as a result. There is a wide welcome for all who come looking for new life in the Sprit, and a strong committed core of Stewards who keep on deepening our spiritual taproot.

Among the Stewards, there has been a slow and healthy turnover. None of the original group of founding members is still active in Stewards, although Emily and Muriel are both present as emeriti. We add or subtract one or two Stewards each year, which means that we have a workable process to supply maturing servant leaders over time. That may be the most important result of our simple process for spiritual formation, from worship to the School of Christian Living, to life together in mission groups and perhaps the call to Stewards, from which the Servant Leadership Team is drawn.

Practicing Ministry in Daily Life

As I come to the end of this account of God's call and Seekers' response, I know that there are other threads I didn't choose to follow. Someone else will have the pleasure of sifting through the creative liturgies that Celebration Circle continues to produce, season after season, year after year. Someone might also be drawn to study the sermons posted on the web, which have come from so many different people over the years. Journals and spiritual reports would be another source for how the Spirit has stalked us, individually and as a community.

Peter preached a sermon that held for me the sound of God's word for Seekers:

> I dream of Seekers Church as a "Learning Lab for Claiming Call," a vocational training center for pilgrims who are on mission in the world; a community for encouragement and accountability. I want us to be a place where we can find the vocational intersection where the forces of gladness and need converge, where we can face our fears with all our imperfect energy and incomplete commitment, where we can provoke each other into love and good deeds that will flow out into the ordinary structures of our lives and beyond.[3]

And so it is.

---

3. November 19, 2006.

APPENDIX 1

Membership Commitment of the Church of the Saviour

Used by Seekers 1977–1982

I come today to join a local expression of the Church, which is the body of those to whom the call of God rests to witness to the grace and truth of God.

I recognize that the function of the Church is to glorify God in adoration and sacrificial service, and to be God's missionary to the world, bearing witness to God's redeeming grace in Jesus Christ.

I believe as did Peter that Jesus is the Christ, the son of the living God.

I unreservedly and with abandon commit my life and destiny to Christ, promising to give him a practical priority in all the affairs of life. I will seek first the kingdom of God and his righteousness.

I commit myself, regardless of the expenditures of time, energy and money, to becoming an informed, mature Christian.

I believe that God is the total owner of my life and resources.

I give God the throne in relation to the material aspects of my life. God is the owner.

I am the ower. Because God is a lavish giver I too shall be lavish and cheerful in my regular gifts.

Realizing that Jesus taught and exemplified a life of love, I will seek to be loving in all relations with other individuals, groups, classes, races and

APPENDIX 1 — *Membership Commitment of the Church of the Saviour*

nations and will seek to be a reconciler, living in a manner which will end all war, personal and public.

I will seek to bring every phase of my life under the Lordship of Christ.

When I move from this place I will join some other expression of the Christian church.

APPENDIX 2

Call of Seekers Church
Offered by Sonya Dyer and Fred Taylor to the C of S Council on April 25, 1976

Our call is to form a seekers community which comes together in *weekly worship* rooted in the biblical faith, with *shared leadership*, for mutual nurture; and disperses with a common commitment to discern and participate with Christ in the basic structures in which we live out our lives.

By "seekers" we mean an intentional fellowship which buys into Christ as the world's and our true life source and into "koinonia" with one another and service to the world as the way to actualize this faith.

By "seekers" we mean not persons who have arrived but persons who are intentionally on the way.

By shared leadership we mean a commitment of all seekers to help our worship flow out of and feed into the community's life situation in both "koinonia" and service. From this we envision the possibility of evoking and giving space to new gifts of preaching, liturgical leadership, creative worship forms, etc.

Our perception of mission includes the basic structures in which we must live out our lives as well as those in which we voluntarily choose to put down our weight—these being *work, primary relationships (family, with one's personally significant others), citizenship and mission group*. The seekers community will be about equipping and supporting one another in all of these areas and achieving a rhythm and balance between them.

APPENDIX 2 — *Call of Seekers Church*

The seekers community would see itself called into God's liberation vision for the world by honestly facing and being involved at those *tension points* which our pluralistic world creates. An example of this would be the demand of blacks, the poor and women, for justice and partnership in a heretofore affluent, white, male-dominated society. An existing example is addressing systems which dehumanize children. Other examples of tension points are differing life styles, marriage and family life and alienation and division within the Christian church. We see these *tension points* as places for individual Christian growth and awareness, as well as collecting points for expression of mission. In order for either to have authenticity and depth, education for liberation which includes *creative working with conflict* is essential.

The faith community is committed to persons of all ages. We see children and youth as a valuable and valued part of our life together and desire their inclusion in our care, our culture and our ministry.

APPENDIX 3

Call of Seekers Church

As Approved by the Church of the Saviour Council, September, 1976

Our call is to be a "seekers community" which comes together in weekly worship rooted in the biblical faith, with shared leadership, and disperses with a common commitment to understand and implement Christian servanthood in the basic structures in which we live out our lives.

By "seekers" we mean an intentional fellowship which sees Christ as our true life source and "koinonia" with one another and genuine self-giving to the world as the way to be alongside Christ today.

By "seekers" we mean not persons who have arrived but persons who are intentionally on the way.

By shared leadership we mean a commitment of all seekers to help our worship flow out of and feed into the community's life situation in both "koinonia" and service. From this we envision the possibility of evoking and giving space to new gifts of preaching, liturgical leadership, creative worship forms, etc.

Our perception of mission includes the normal structures of our daily lives work, family and primary relationships, citizenship and mission group. The seekers community will be about equipping and supporting one another in all of these areas and achieving a rhythm and balance between them.

The Seekers community sees itself called into Christ's ministry of deliverance from bondage to freedom in every personal and corporate expression.

APPENDIX 3 — *Call of Seekers Church*

The Seekers community is committed to persons of all ages. We see children and youth as a valuable and valued part of our life together and desire their inclusion in our care, our ministry and our life together.

APPENDIX 4

Seekers' Call (1989)

Our call is to be a "seekers community" which comes together in weekly worship rooted in the biblical faith, with shared leadership, and disperses with a common commitment to understand and implement Christian servanthood in the basic structures in which we live out our lives.

By "seekers community" we mean an intentional body which sees Christ as our true life source. Koinonia with one another and genuine self-giving to the world are the ways we can be in Christ today. Seekers are not persons who have arrived, but persons who are intentionally on the way.

By shared leadership we mean empowering the gifts of women and men to help our worship flow out of and feed into the life of the community. We are committed to evoking and giving space to new gifts of preaching, liturgical leadership, creative worship forms giving, mission and other acts of faith.

For us, Christian servanthood is based on empowering others within the normal structures of our daily lives (work, family, primary relationships, and citizenship), as well as through special structures for service and witness. **We desire and welcome participation in Seekers of women and men of every race and sexual orientation.** In Seekers Church, we will equip and support one another in all of these areas and seek a balance between them.

The seekers community sees itself called into Christ's ministry of deliverance from bondage to freedom in every personal and corporate expression. **We recognize the value of each individual and seek to heal any wounds of discrimination inflicted by our society and church.**

APPENDIX 4 — *Seekers' Call (1989)*

The Seekers community is committed to persons of all ages. We see children and youth as a valuable and valued part of our life together and desire their inclusion in our care, our ministry and our life together.

Note: additions in boldface.

APPENDIX 5

Stewards Commitment Statement
Adopted in 1983; Revised 2001

I come today to make my commitment *as a Steward of* Seekers Church, a Christian Community in the tradition of the Church of the Saviour, linked with the people of God throughout the ages.

Along with the disciples, we worship God as triune being.

Along with the disciples, we believe:

- That the Creator–father and mother to us all, ground of being–loves, sustains and calls us;
- That Jesus is the Christ, who calls us to a ministry of love and justice;
- That the Holy Spirit, as the empowering presence and breath of God, confronts and inspires us to do God's work in the world.

We believe that we are all ministers of the Church, which is both universal, grace-filled body of Christ, and fragile earthen vessel.

I commit to:
- Be a faithful witness to God's presence among us;
- Nurture my relationship with God and Seekers through specific disciplines;
- Care for the whole of creation, beginning with the natural environment;
- Foster justice and be in solidarity with the poor;
- Work for the ending of all war, personal and public;

APPENDIX 5 — *Stewards Commitment Statement*

- Share responsibility for the spiritual growth of persons of all ages in my community;
- Take responsibility for the organizational health of Seekers Church;
- Respond joyfully with my life, as the grace of God gives me freedom.

When I move from this place I will join some other expression of Christ's church.

APPENDIX 6

Disciplines of the Stewards
Adopted in May 1987; Revised in 2001

Becoming a mature member of the Body of Christ grows from the practice of our love of Jesus Christ, of others and of ourselves. Stewards embrace common disciplines which express that love and which are necessary for personal growth in Christ and for the building of the faith community. The common disciplines are:

- Attending Sunday worship, usually with Seekers Church;
- Observing daily quiet time – prayer, scripture reading, and reflection or journaling. Scripture reading is usually guided by the ecumenical lectionary which is also used for our Sunday worship;
- Giving proportionately of income to Seekers Church, beginning at ten percent;
- Making a silent retreat once a year, if possible with Seekers;
- Participating in an ongoing mission group with two or more Stewards, for living out the person's chosen ministry, for building the Church, and for accountability in spiritual growth;
- Being accountable for the spiritual journey in a regular written report to the spiritual guide of the group;
- Attending Stewards' meetings regularly;
- Expressing commitment to discovery and use of gifts, to education and growth in the faith, and to the pastoring and support of the community as a whole in the ongoing life of Seekers Church;

APPENDIX 6 — *Disciplines of the Stewards*

- Reviewing the Stewards' commitment with one's group or another Steward and spending an hour in meditation prior to Recommitment Sunday in October.

APPENDIX 7

General Membership Statements

Sonya's *potential* statement for all Seekers (1978)

I will seek to bring every phase of my life under the Lordship of Christ. As a member of the Seekers Community, I pledge myself to live out this commitment:

- by seeking to learn what it means to be church in the world today;
- by intentionally including all facets of my life in this ongoing process; and
- by being flexible and willing to embrace the new and the creative in our own midst and in the world.

When I move from this place I will join some other expression of the Christian Church.

For Recommitment, October 20, 1991, the staff team took unilateral action to make membership possible for anyone who wanted to identify themselves with Seekers to stand and say:

- *I am a Seeker.*
- *The Seekers Church of the Church of the Saviour is my church.*
- *I acknowledge that I am called by God to be part of this community.*
- *As part of the community, I have work to do.*

APPENDIX 7 — *General Membership Statements*

- *As part of the community, I have joy and pain to share, and joy and pain to bear.*

- *As part of the community, I am a growing Christian.*

- *I will be intentional and accountable about naming my relationship to the community and living out my intentions.*

Fall 2001: Revised General Membership Statement

I am a Seeker. I come today to affirm my relationship with this Christian community in the tradition of the Church of the Saviour, linked with the people of God through the ages.

As a member of this church, I will deepen my relationships in this local expression of the Body of Christ, sharing my gifts from God with others who worship with Seekers Church, and in the wider world. I will:

- *Nurture my relationship with God and Seekers Church through spiritual disciplines;*

- *Care for the whole of creation, including the natural environment;*

- *Foster justice and be in solidarity with the poor;*

- *Work for the end of all war, both public and private; and*

- *Respond joyfully with my life, as the grace of God gives me freedom.*

APPENDIX 7 — *General Membership Statements*

Children's Membership Statement written by David Lloyd for Recommitment Sunday in 2006:

I promise

- *to learn about God by coming to this church,*
- *to take care of the air, water, and earth, and to love the animals, birds and fish in it,*
- *to help poor people,*
- *to try to get along with my family, my friends and others, and*
- *to say "yes" to God as I grow.*

APPENDIX 8

Books by Seekers

Bankson, Marjory Zoet. *Braided Streams: Esther and a Woman's Way of Growing.* Minneapolis: Augsburg, 2005.
———. *Creative Aging: Rethinking Retirement and Non-Retirement in a Changing World.* Woodstock VT: Skylight Paths, 2011.
———. "The Power of Commitment: It Can Happen Anywhere." In *Best Practices from America's Best Churches*, edited by Paul Wilkes, 253–69. New York: Paulist, 2003.
———. *Seasons of Friendship: Naomi and Ruth as a Model for Relationship.* Rev. ed. Minneapolis: Augsburg, 2005.
———. *The Call to the Soul: Six Stages of Spiritual Development.* Minneapolis: Augsburg, 2005.
———. *The Soulwork of Clay: A Hands-On Approach to Spirituality.* Woodstock, VT: Skylight Paths, 2008.
Conover, Pat. *Transgender Good News.* Silver Spring, MD: New Wineskins, 2002.
Lipp, Muriel. *Secrets of the Forest.* Minocqua, WI: NorthWord, 1995.
McMakin, Jacqueline, and Sonya Dyer. *Working from the Heart: A Guide to Cultivating the Soul at Work.* San Francisco: HarperSanFrancisco, 1993.
Powell, Mary Clare. *The Widow.* Washington, DC: Anchor, 1981.
———, and Annie Cheatham. *This Way Daybreak Comes: Women's Values and the Future.* Philadelphia: New Society, 1986.
Sokolove, Deborah, and Peter Bankson. *Calling on God: Inclusive Christian Prayers for Three Years of Sundays.* Woodstock, VT: Skylight Paths, 2014.
———. "Changing Roles: Becoming Orphaned." In *Wising Up: Ritual Resources for Women of Faith in Their Journey of Aging*, edited by Kathy Black and Heather Murray Elkins. Cleveland: Pilgrim, 2005.
———. "More Than Words." In *New Feminist Christianity*, edited by Mary Hunt and Diann Neu, 182–89. Woodstock, VT: Skylight Paths, 2010.
———. *Sanctifying Art: Inviting Conversation between Artists, Theologians, and the Church.* Eugene, OR: Cascade Books, 2013.
Taylor, Fred. *Roll Away the Stone: Saving America's Children.* Great Falls, VA: Information International, 1999.

APPENDIX 9

Questions for Emerging Churches

1. FAMILY HERITAGE

1. For C of S, the call was to make disciples capable of having the same relationship with God that Jesus had. Known as *"the inward/outward journey,"* yearly recommitment encouraged people to take their response seriously. What is the call or vision for your church? How is that shared with the congregation?

2. What is the mission or purpose for your church? What are the structures (like mission groups) to carry out that mission?

3. What is the path to full participation in your community? Is there some way to move from visitor to informed membership and eventually into leadership?

4. What are the places of growth, tension, or change that might lead to new forms?

2. IN THE BEGINNING

1. The call statement at Seekers is divided into three parts: personal disciplines, community stewardship, and a broad definition of ministry in daily life. Does your church have a mission statement? If not, what would you say is the core of God's call for you?

2. How does your budget express the mission of your church?

APPENDIX 9 — *Questions for Emerging Churches*

3. What did equal pay for different amounts of work suggest about the leadership team at Seekers?

3. SHARED LEADERSHIP

1. Is there a primary theological reference for worship in your church? Would you say it is God? Jesus? Christ or the Holy Spirit? What difference does that make?
2. What are the visual symbols that express your theological stance? Who designed them? How permanent or transitory are they?
3. How is decision making handled in your church? Who belongs to that body? How are they selected? Is this related in any way to the primary theological framework for worship?

4. NURTURING THE WHOLE COMMUNITY

1. How does your church determine which missions to support?
2. What are the structures for ongoing spiritual formation in your church?
3. How does tension or opposition develop resilience and clarity for leaders in your church?

5. MONEY AS A WORKING THEOLOGY

1. What are the values that underlie your church's operating budget and investment policy? Who makes those decisions? How much information is shared with the congregation?
2. How might you invite key members of your congregation to write and share a money autobiography? What are some of the barriers you might encounter? Are there other ways to demystify the power of money in your congregation?
3. The Growing Edge Fund has been a fruitful source of encouragement for creative risk taking at Seekers. Can you imagine a similar source of

APPENDIX 9—*Questions for Emerging Churches*

support in your congregation? What would it look like? Who might be interested in publicizing it? Or partnering with recipients?

6. BELIEFS THAT BIND US TOGETHER

1. Does your church have some kind of doctrinal statement (like the Apostle's Creed)? How might the language be changed to make it more inclusive? What would it take to have that adopted?

2. If you were describing your church in a brochure, what are the main characteristics?

3. Do people in your church make some kind of public commitment for membership? If not, what do you think is the common understanding of shared responsibility? Are children and other "unproductive" members included?

4. Does your church belong to a wider network, like Seekers within Church of the Saviour? What value does an association or denomination have? What are the downsides of such an association?

7. OPEN PULPIT AT SEEKERS

1. Has your community experienced a period of growth? How would your community identify new leadership needs?

2. How might your governing body deal with the question about spiritual depth vs. administrative capabilities? Seekers tried to call forth a spiritual director for the core members by drawing on the monastic tradition and naming an abbot. That did not prove to be effective. What has your experience been?

3. What difference does it make to have one voice or many different voices in the pulpit? What would that mean for your congregation? What would it mean for you?

4. When the core members decided not to hire a specialist, but to call forth a team for "leadership of the whole," what did that mean for Seekers? What would it mean for your community?

APPENDIX 9 — *Questions for Emerging Churches*

8. TEAM LEADERSHIP

1. If the call or mission statement of your church was to be changed, how would that happen?
2. Do you have guidelines for using funds for particular purposes, like bequests or external giving? How are those guidelines developed? Who might be involved?
3. What is the membership statement in your church? Are there additional requirements for those who hold the core structure? How does one move from being a visitor to a core member in your congregation?
4. What would you say the "stress points" are in your church? Who would know about those? Who might be involved in counseling couples with marital problems or boundary issues within the congregation?

9. NEW WINESKINS

1. In the timeline of your church, what have been the major turning points or defining events?
2. If you were to reimagine your community, what are ten key issues you would address?
3. How have personal events, like baptisms, marriages, and burials, strengthened the life of your community? Are there other events, like birthdays or anniversaries, that nurture connections?

10. HOLDING THE TENSION

1. How do you experience the tension between "doing business" and "building relationships"? What are some of the other polarities, like commitment vs. inclusion, or spiritual vs. practical, that seem to hold creative tension in your church?
2. What are the functions of your governing board? How do they tend the spiritual life of your community? How does that compare with the functions of Stewards at Seekers?

APPENDIX 9 — *Questions for Emerging Churches*

3. Has your church made a decision to purchase property? If so, how was that done? What would you say about making an investment from your total wealth in your community?

11. NEW LEADERSHIP EMERGES

1. What is the process in your community for confirming someone's call to leadership?
2. If you have experienced the transition from founder to the next generation of leadership in your church, business, or volunteer agency, what are some of the learnings you have to share?
3. How might Seekers have handled the transition to a servant leadership team more skillfully? What are the qualities that you look for in leadership? How are people schooled to be alert and aware as followers?

12. MANNA IN THE DESERT

1. What is the role of worship in times of personal or community crisis? Do you have some experience with that? Can you describe the particular parts of worship that have been important for you?
2. On your pastoral staff, what adjustments have you experienced when a new person joins an existing team? What difference does it make to have a team of generalists instead of hiring specialists for particular jobs?
3. Creating the large mosaic for the front of the building was a common activity with a highly symbolic outcome. What others activities might have had such a unifying effect?

13. HOME AT LAST!

1. What kind of neighborhood outreach does your church have? Who does that? How is it organized? What have been the results?
2. Seekers identifies itself as "living at the crossroads of commitment and inclusion." What would you say are the axial coordinates for your congregation?

3. When discontent arises in your church, how is that handled? How do you listen to the "underbelly" voices? Is there one person, or a group of people, who are skilled at conflict resolution?

14. PRACTICING MINISTRY IN DAILY LIFE

1. What new missions have developed in the life of your church in the past five years? How has that happened? Who might have been the focus of a new call?

2. How does spiritual formation happen in your church? Who is responsible for leadership and guidance? How do you deal with resistance to the inner journey, personal and corporate?

3. What are the structures for your "outward journey" as a community? Informal support for individual efforts? Formal structures for corporate mission?

4. What are the financial considerations for mission in your church? How is corporate debt addressed? Who decides how your collective resources will be spent?

5. If there is a sudden change in the leadership structure (like Kate's death), how do you select a new leader or leaders? Do you select from inside your community? Or solicit leadership from outside of the community? What does that say about your structures for spiritual formation? How might that be addressed?

Bibliography

Bonhoeffer, Dietrich. *Life Together.* New York: Harper & Row, 1954.
Cosby, N. Gordon. *By Grace Transformed.* New York: Crossroad, 1999.
———. *Handbook for Mission Groups.* Waco, TX: Word, 1975.
Greenleaf, Robert. "On Being a Seekers in the Late 20th Century." *Friends Journal*, September 15, 1975.
———. *Servant Leadership: A Journey into the Nature of Legitimate Power and Greatness.* New York: Paulist, 1977.
Minutes from monthly Stewards meetings, 1976–2013. Seekers Church Archives.
O'Connor, Elizabeth. *Call to Commitment.* New York: Harper & Row, 1963.
———. *Cry Pain, Cry Hope.* Waco, TX: Word, 1987.
———. *Eighth Day of Creation.* Waco, TX: Word, 1971.
———. *Journey Inward, Journey Outward.* New York: Harper & Row, 1969.
———. *Letters to Scattered Pilgrims.* New York: Harper & Row, 1979.
———. *Our Many Selves.* New York: Harper & Row, 1971.
———. *Search for Silence.* Waco, TX: Word, 1972.
———. *Servant Leaders, Servant Structures.* Washington, DC: Servant Leadership School, 1991.
———. *The New Community.* New York: Harper & Row, 1976.
———. "What We Need Is More Saints." *Faith at Work*, October–November, 1963.
Taylor, Fred. *Roll Away the Stone: Saving America's Children.* Great Falls, VA: Information International, 1999.

Index

autobiography, 3, 45, 69, 166
Amoss, Billy, 76, 106, 131
Amoss, Kate, 125, 131
Arms, Ron, 62, 68, 75, 91–2, 100
Artist's mission group, 27, 34–5, 96, 126–7
Bankson, Peter, 35–7, 59, 63–5, 67, 69–71, 76, 80–2, 87, 90, 94, 100, 102–4, 106–115, 118–21, 123, 125, 128–30, 132, 139, 142, 144–7
Barber, Roy, 91, 96, 118, 141
Bayer, Bob, 52, 63–4, 69, 71, 80
Benson (Gilbert), Emily, 6, 23, 36, 47, 51–3, 55, 120, 129, 146
bequest, 44, 49, 76, 143, 168
body of Christ, 1, 3, 9, 14, 31, 37, 52, 120, 128, 157, 159, 162
Bokamoso Youth Center, 96, 118, 141
Bonhoeffer, Dietrich, 2, 3
Branner, Bill, 1, 2, 27, 79, 90
Broken & Beloved, 138, 141
Building Development Team (BDT), 104, 107–08, 121, 127, 130
Burton, Ken, 113
care packs, 141–2
Carroll Café, 137
Celebration Circle (CC), 37–8, 54, 59, 61, 70, 71, 74, 87, 90–91, 100, 104–5, 125–6, 131, 133, 138, 146–7
chalice, 24
Church of the Servant Jesus, 86, 94, 122
Christ House, 56, 72, 80, 85, 94, 142
Conover, Pat, 63–4, 66–7, 71, 74, 83, 88–93, 98, 107–10, 164
Cook, John, 82

Cosby, Gordon, 1- 3, 12, 14, 17, 19, 21–2, 27, 35–6, 40–1, 44, 53, 55, 57, 70, 78–83, 85–6, 91, 94, 99, 121–2, 138–9, 142–3
Cosby, Mary, 1, 79, 94, 121, 142
Cudlipp, Kate, 69, 72, 81–2, 99, 100, 102–3, 106, 109–12, 115, 118, 122, 125, 132–3, 137–8, 142, 144
Dahlin, Cynthia, 100, 129
Dayspring, 2, 3, 7–9, 11–13, 16, 19, 32, 41, 44–5, 50, 56–7, 67, 72, 75–6, 78–82, 85–8, 94, 121, 129, 137–8, 140, 142–4
Dickerson, Jim, 49, 56, 64
Dunamis, 16, 19, 56
Dyer, Manning, 15, 96, 100
Dyer, Sonya, 6, 9–10, 12, 14–22, 25–7, 29, 31–5, 37–9, 43–4, 467–9, 51–5, 57–60, 62–5, 70, 73–4, 76–7, 80–2, 86–7, 90, 93, 96, 99–101, 110, 112, 114, 116, 124, 131–3, 151
Eighth Day, 17, 19, 33, 56, 80, 85
Engle, Jane, 113
Equal Rights Amendment (ERA), 33, 39
Eyes to See (Is2C), 137–8, 145–6
Faithful Servant Trust Fund, 79, 85, 142
Farnham, Suzanne, 99
Festival Center, 55–6, 72–3, 79, 82, 138
Fisher, Katie, 131, 136–7
Financial Oversight Group (FOG), 90, 97, 130
For Love of Children (FLOC), 53–5, 59–60, 62, 81, 100–101, 140
Gateway, 19, 72, 79, 80, 85
gift, 33–4, 96, 104, 110, 122, 127, 132
Granberg-Michaelson, Wes, 11

173

Index

Gratton, Carolyn, 123
Greenleaf, Robert, 10–12, 21, 62, 115, 145
Growing Edge Fund, 46–7, 68, 74, 76–7, 90–91, 119, 141, 166
Guatemala, 118, 132
Guenther, Margaret, 123
Holmes, Paul, 34
Hubers, Carolyn & Tom, 109, 144
Hudson, Trevor, 34
Hope and a Home, 6–7, 53–4, 100
inclusion, 25, 29, 52, 60, 63–4, 71, 91, 106–7, 127–8, 139, 152, 154
intentional community, 21–2, 29, 42, 46, 50, 62, 73–4, 99, 128, 151, 153, 155, 162
Interplay, 77, 131–2, 137
inward/outward journey, 7, 69, 121, 141, 143, 165
Johnson, Sue, 131
Jubilee, 8, 9, 11, 17, 19, 44, 56, 80, 85, 94, 138
Koinonia, 59, 130, 138–9, 146, 151, 153, 155
Lake of the Saints, 57, 87, 129
Lazarus House, 72, 79, 80, 85
Learners & Teachers (L&T), 36–7, 83, 93, 111, 131, 138–9, 146
Lipp, Muriel, 2, 9–10, 16–17, 41, 47, 84, 109, 129
Living Water, 129, 138, 140
Lloyd, David, 25, 36, 47–8, 53, 67, 76, 106, 110, 114, 122, 125, 163
liturgy, liturgist, 22, 25, 32, 54, 57, 85, 105, 113–4, 125–6, 139
Manna, 43–4, 49, 56, 64, 71, 76, 89, 97, 108, 117, 119, 121, 123, 127, 138, 143
Marcus, Jeanne, 109–15, 117–18, 120, 124, 129–31
McClanen, Don, 44
McClurg, Kayla, 138
McMurray, Mollie, 88
ministry in daily life, 16, 20–1, 28, 35, 46, 52, 66, 85, 121, 127–8, 136, 141, 146
ministry team, 61–64, 68–70, 74, 116

Mission Support Group (MSG), 35, 84, 138
Nemore, Trish, 83, 145–6
New Community Church, 49, 53, 56, 62, 72, 79, 80, 85, 105
New Lands, 9–12, 16, 19, 21, 36, 38, 40, 45, 57, 79
O'Connor, Elizabeth, 3–4, 6–7, 23, 27, 33, 36, 38, 40, 53, 70, 80, 86, 96, 124
Ogle, Kevin. 105
open pulpit, 58, 62, 64, 70, 121, 126, 135, 139
ordination, 19, 33, 39, 52–3, 61, 70, 73, 91
Palidofsky, Jesse, 99, 106, 127, 137
pastoring, 12, 15, 22, 54, 58, 60, 65, 110–12, 117, 123, 132, 159
Phillips, Martha, 126
Potter's House, 4, 6–9, 11–12, 14–5, 17, 19, 35, 46–7, 54–57, 71–2, 79–81, 85, 138
Powell, Mary Clare, 16, 46, 55
Price, Bill, 79
recommitment, 1, 3, 7, 17, 19, 29, 51, 54, 73, 98, 107
Rolling Ridge, 76, 99, 106, 127, 140
Rouse, Jim, 55
Sarah's Circle, 56–7
School of Christian Living (SCL), 3, 7–8, 12, 25, 28, 30, 36, 38, 44, 56, 67, 71, 73–4, 78, 89, 91, 106, 128, 131, 140, 146
Schultz, Kay, 64–5, 69, 71, 76, 80–1, 99
Schultz, John, 71, 99, 119
Seat, Brenda, 87, 100, 104, 106, 114–5, 118, 129, 132, 144–6
Seat, Keith, 87–8, 104, 107, 117, 121–2, 127, 138, 143
Second Wave, 41–2
servant leadership, 10, 54, 146, 169
Servant Leadership School, 55, 73
Servant Leadership Team (SLT), 115–7, 124, 127, 135, 139, 144–6
silent retreat, 2, 7, 11, 16, 29, 32, 85, 88, 102, 129, 159
Silverstone, Jeffrey, 75, 90, 106

Index

Silverstone, Margreta (Voskuilen), 75, 125
Sokolove, Deborah, 91, 104, 114, 120–1, 125, 130, 139
Strand, Mike, 129
spiritual growth, 8, 29, 36, 73, 98, 131, 158–9
Taylor, Fred, 5–6, 9–10, 12, 14–22, 24–6, 31, 33–5, 37–41, 43–4, 46–9, 52–5, 58–63, 65, 70, 79, 110, 112, 139, 151
Time & Space mission group, 130, 136, 138, 146
tithing, 15, 29, 43, 47–9, 74, 83, 133
Vail, Liz, 27, 33–4, 41, 46–7, 52, 77, 90
Wellspring, 2, 8, 11, 16, 19, 23, 32, 40–1, 44–5, 55, 67, 69, 72, 83, 85, 87, 105, 121, 123, 132, 143
Westerhoff, John, 25
Wilson, Bill, 120
Winstead, Adelaide, 53
Winterveldt, South Africa, 34, 96, 118
Wren, Brian, 125
Wysockey-Johnson, Kathryn, 120, 123
Yakushiji, Glen, 104, 106, 120–1, 137

www.ingramcontent.com/pod-product-compliance
Lightning Source LLC
Chambersburg PA
CBHW071453150426
43191CB00008B/1337